S0-CFY-150

Spiritual Body Building

Manual

Kim A. Johnson

The Ministerial Association
General Conference of Seventh-day Adventists
Silver Spring, MD 20904

Copyright © 1997
General Conference of Seventh-day Adventists Ministerial Association

PRINTED IN U.S.A.
by Review and Herald Graphics
Hagerstown, MD 21740

Unless otherwise indicated, Bible texts quoted in this series are from the King James Version or the New King James Version. NKJV copyright 1979, 1980, 1982, Thomas Nelson, Inc., Publishers. Used by permission.

Kim A. Johnson, associate ministerial director and associate treasurer of Northern New England Conference. He has a Masters of Divinity from the Seventh-day Theological Seminary, Andrews University, Berrien Springs, Michigan.

The author assumes full responsibility for all facts and quotations cited in this book.

ISBN 1-57847-008-0

Contents

I. Introduction

1. The Vision

Welcome to Spiritual Body Building! You are beginning a great adventure. Body Building is a series of 16 small-group lessons designed to implant a new vision in church members' hearts of how to be church. During the past three years the lessons have been used by many churches. The lessons help Seventh-day Adventists look at themselves and their church through new glasses. The ultimate goal is to develop a nurturing, spiritual community that produces maturing disciples for Christ.

Some people appreciate manuals, others tolerate them, still others ignore them altogether. How about you? When you bought that new exercise equipment from Wal-Mart, did you rip open the package and start assembling the pieces without looking at the manual? Did you think it was a sign of weakness or mechanical ineptitude to follow the instructions? That's the course I usually take, but inevitably I wind up with leftover parts or, worse, not enough. Or the gazinker gets connected to the dumbfozzle instead of the ruckernick. Anyway, experience has taught me that manuals *can* be useful. My hope is, obviously, that you'll take time to **read through this manual before you begin your small group**. When you go in for surgery you hope the surgeon has read the manual, and your Body Building Group members will expect the same from you. This manual is in many ways a compilation of what has worked for others. Instead of trying to reinvent the wheel, you can benefit from their mistakes and successes and do even better. Take what is here, rework it to fit your own personality and circumstances, and look forward to a wonderful journey with God.

2. Rationale

The underlying rationale and purpose for the Body Building Lessons is highlighted in the following two graphics, "Church Life Cycle" and "Two Models of Church." Refer to these graphics as you read through the explanations that follow each one. These graphics also appear in the final lesson in this series, "The Value of Vision." The first graphic, entitled "Church Life Cycle," depicts the value of vision.

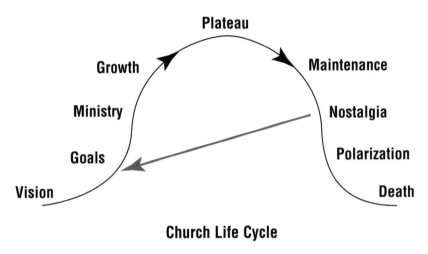

Church Life Cycle

(Modified from *Reviving the Plateaued Church*, by R. D. Baker, Truman Brown, Jr., Robert Dale, p. 6)

Local congregations usually begin with a small group of people who have a **vision** for starting a church in their area. They set **goals**, organize for **ministry**, and **growth** results. Perhaps, after several years, the church unfortunately **plateaus** and may settle into a **maintenance** mode. Not too awful, but not too exciting either. They begin sliding down the slippery slope. There may be no decline in numbers, but spiritually things are slowly rotting from within. Next, **nostalgia** sets in, and the members begin to recount the "good old days." "Remember when we used to get big crowds for Ingathering?" "Remember when the youth used to turn out in droves for Friday night MV?" The members may then become **polarized** by forming little cliques. The church is like spiritual swiss cheese, full of holes. The building is still standing. The people still come every week.

They still hold VBS and cooking schools, but the vitality has drained away. Church is predictable. They are nearing spiritual **death**.

The problem is usually that the old vision has faded and lost its power. The wrong approach is to try and climb back up the slippery slope. The answer is to go back to **vision**. The Body Building Lessons are specifically designed to enable church members to **discover God's vision** for them and their church.

The second graphic, "Two Models of Church," is somewhat more involved. It is important that you pause here for a few moments to look it over and read the explanation that follows. Properly understood, this graphic reveals how vital the concepts in the Body Building Lessons really are.

The Information Model (refer to "Two Models" chart on the next page)

On the left is the Information Model of church. It puts primary emphasis on **spreading correct biblical information** to as many people as you can, as fast as you can. The church sees its main purpose as preaching and teaching the Gospel, the three angels' messages, and other biblical truths. Out of that root perspective there unfortunately emerges the following list of priorities and consequences, the fruit:

- **Information/Task**—Information sharing becomes the primary goal. We may not describe such an emphasis in this way, but our actions indicate our priorities.
- **Programs/Media**—It is logical, then, to depend more and more on methods that will get the information out the fastest, such as mass media and programs.
- **Reaping**—Getting people to say yes to the information and accept it becomes our major focus, so reaping or getting decisions is paramount.
- **Few Spiritual Gifts**—The heavy emphasis on information sharing and reaping leaves many people with planting, sowing, and nurturing gifts out in the cold, feeling like they don't fit in or are not valued.

•**Professionals**—We increasingly depend on the religious professionals (pastors, evangelists, etc.) who can explain the information best.

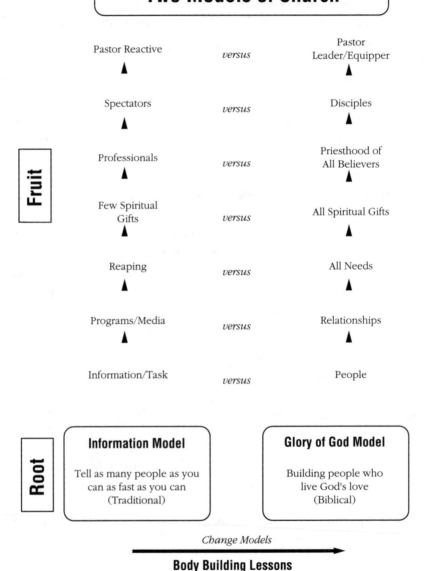

Two Models of Church

Pastor Reactive ▲	*versus*	Pastor Leader/Equipper ▲
Spectators ▲	*versus*	Disciples ▲
Professionals ▲	*versus*	Priesthood of All Believers ▲
Few Spiritual Gifts ▲	*versus*	All Spiritual Gifts ▲
Reaping ▲	*versus*	All Needs ▲
Programs/Media ▲	*versus*	Relationships ▲
Information/Task	*versus*	People

Fruit

Root

Information Model

Tell as many people as you can as fast as you can
(Traditional)

Glory of God Model

Building people who live God's love
(Biblical)

Change Models

Body Building Lessons

- **Spectators**—The members develop a spectator mentality because they do not see themselves as vital to success.
- **Pastor Reactive**—Because the many gifts of the Spirit are not activated, the ministry load falls squarely on the pastor's shoulders. He adopts a reactive mode, like a plumber who spends all day fixing leaks.

All of these consequences flow logically and tragically from the underlying root paradigm of the Information Model of church. Information (biblical truth) is of course vital, but it is a means to an end, not an end in itself. This model is not "wrong." It is simply far too narrow, and such an imbalance can have a very negative effect on church life. God has a much larger vision in mind.

The Glory of God Model

The Glory of God Model emphasizes building people to the glory of God; that is, people who the Spirit enables to love. It is about biblical disciple making. It includes biblical information and truth to be sure, but so much more. The positive consequences and priorities that flow naturally out of this very different model include these:

- **People**—Building people becomes the key to being church. The emphasis is not only on *what* we know but, more importantly, on *who* we are. It is broad, holistic, and balanced.
- **Relationships**—The ultimate focus is squarely on relationships, within the church and without.
- **All Needs**—We are now interested in meeting whatever needs people may have in order to help them become whole.
- **All Spiritual Gifts**—In order to meet the great variety of people needs, we must activate all the gifts of the Spirit.
- **Priesthood of All Believers**—Activating all the gifts means that we must take seriously the vital biblical teaching of the priesthood of all believers.
- **Disciples**—Because of the emphasis on holism and everyone being a priest, our goal becomes not just baptisms but producing mature disciples for Christ.

- **Pastor Leader/Equipper**—Now that the gifts and ministries of the laity are activated, the pastor can become the specialist God designed as a leader/equipper.

It is the Glory of God Model that captures the biblical vision best. Notice that it is rather useless to try to change one of the fruit from the left side of the "Two Models" chart to the right side without first changing the fundamental understanding of church that is in people's heads.

Unless we alter people's underlying values and philosophy, change will not make much sense and will be seen as either a threat or just one more transient program. We need to deal with the root before the fruit. Remember, "Change the *mind* before you change the *method.*" Unless we focus on members' underlying views of God and church, changes in methods will be like the rubber band that stretches out for a while and then snaps back as soon as you let go. **These 16 lessons and small-group experiences are specifically designed to help people shift the roots of their thinking from the Information Model to the more complete Glory of God Model**. Change can then follow as a logical consequence.

A final way of looking at the purpose of the Body Building Lessons is to compare our church members' spiritual experience to a hot air balloon. The Holy Spirit, like the hot air inside, is trying to lift that balloon off the ground, but several strong ropes hold the balloon to the ground. Those ropes represent distorted or limited thinking on the part of our members. Each of the Body Building Lessons is designed to cut one of those ropes. Ideally, if enough ropes are cut, the Holy Spirit can lift our people to new heights in their Christian experience, individually and as a church family.

3. Lesson Summary

The Body Building Lessons all come in one participant workbook. The paging is continuous so members can find each lesson from the table of contents. Usually groups study one lesson each week. The following is a lesson summary:

1. What is Church—Part A
The often-neglected but critical subject of defining what we mean by "church." Group members look at the scriptural images of the bride, living stones, and flock.

2. What Is Church—Part B
The biblical images of church as body, salt, army, and family.

3. You Are A Minister!
The vital concept of the priesthood of all believers.

4. Hey, Pastor!
The pastor's biblical job description and its practical implications.

5. High-Rise Christians
Lessons 5, 6, 7, and 8 examine the topic of spiritual gifts. This lesson shows how spiritual gifts provide self-worth, a sense of belonging, a call to ministry, and freedom from guilt. It also explores how believers can play a critical role in continuing the ministry of Christ.

6. The Joy of Gifts
Spiritual gifts and natural talents, fruit of the Spirit, gifts and roles, as well as definitions of the gifts of Hospitality, Helps, Intercession, Encouragement, Discernment, Faith, and Mercy.

7. Opening Your Gifts
How to discover your spiritual gifts. This chapter also defines the gifts of Knowledge, Wisdom, Leadership, Administration, Teaching, and Healing.

8. Gift Wrap
Wraps up our study on gifts by examining gift projection, gift exaltation, gift exclusiveness, and gift immaturity. Also defines the gifts of Craftsmanship, Giving, Music, Evangelism, Pastor, and Prophecy.

9. The Orchestra

How to bring about fundamental, lasting renewal by paying attention to organism problems and solutions.

10. The Kiss

The assurance of salvation.

11. The Disciple's Heart

Spiritual growth and maturity.

12. The Telescope

Why God gave us our doctrines. Shows how doctrines should be a means to an end—producing mature, loving disciples—rather than an end in themselves.

13. Lovesharing

A fresh look at witnessing. Christ's unbeatable method for reaching the lost.

14. Disciple Makers

Jesus' multiplication strategy for developing mature disciples.

15. Just Imagine!

Explores the thrilling Glory of God model of church and its implications for today.

16. The Value of Vision

How both a church vision and a personal mission statement can help answer the important question, "Where do we go from here?"

4. Body Building At A Glance

Body Building consists of two main parts: (1) the small-group meetings and (2) the outcomes, or results, that can flow from that experience. **The emphasis is on small groups with a purpose**. For this process to be effective, it will require both group facilitation skills and a well-thought-out plan. Both aspects are covered in considerable detail in this manual. Sections II, III, and IV of the manual deal mainly with how to use the 16 lessons to create a successful small group. Sections V and VI focus on how the small-group experience can produce certain intentional results. There are several kinds of outcomes from which to choose. The manual ends with two appendices:

Appendix A: Group Guidelines and Covenant.
Appendix B: Assessment Guides for Ministry Placement.

5. Understanding Your Purpose

Body Building Groups can be an excellent opportunity for enhancing spiritual growth and developing a sense of community. Ideally you will view these groups as the *beginning* of an ongoing *process* of change rather than as an isolated *event* on a busy church calendar. Pastors often find themselves running from one round of programs and seminars to the next, trying to discover the right one for turning things around. **Body Building can be different because it deals with underlying causes and philosophy**. Rather than investing in a series of disconnected efforts, you can lay the foundation for consistent progress. You can bring continuity to your church's ministry by getting at the root of God's purposes.

Your experience with Body Building will be greatly enhanced if you do what Stephen Covey calls "**beginning with the end in mind**." That means you think through what you want the result to be before you even start your Body Building Group. We often do this in other areas of life. If you want to have a great vacation, you usually try to figure out where you want to go and what you want to see before you leave the driveway. Otherwise you wind up meandering all over the countryside, never quite sure where to go next. The same is true when you build a house. Before you have the lumber delivered and begin hammering nails, you do some planning and get the blueprints together. Otherwise, even though you have fine material and put in many long hours, you could easily end up with nothing more than a weird-looking shack. It is critical that you understand your purpose in using the Body Building Lessons. Please don't rush into your Body Building Group without understanding what you are trying to accomplish. Study the possible outcomes presented here and plan wisely.

Because the series deals with people's fundamental understanding of God's vision for church, several potential outcomes might be achieved:

1. Fostering personal spiritual renewal
2. Developing a shared vision among leaders and influencers.
3. Reshaping the church culture by positively influencing values and attitudes.
4. Assimilating both new and veteran members into the body of Christ.
5. Transforming existing groups within the church.
6. Giving birth to new small groups.
7. Becoming the launching pad for a Ministry Development Process.

Obviously these items overlap, but separating them helps you target more clearly and intentionally what you are trying to accomplish. You may focus on any of these outcomes at the same time. **Which outcomes and what combination you choose is up to you.** They are not sequential. The lessons attempt to provide both clear direction and maximum flexibility. For a more in-depth explanation of each of these items, see sections V and VI in this manual. Those sections will help you clarify your purpose before beginning your Body Building Group.

Some outcomes require more organization and planning than others. Which outcomes you choose depends to a large extent on your leadership resources and the current condition of your church.

Leadership Resources: Leadership is the key to most endeavors. How far a church can advance depends largely on the number of leaders, their skill, and vision. We urge pastors to work with a leadership team, but at the outset much of the responsibility for getting the ball rolling with Body Building will inevitably fall on the pastor's shoulders. He or she will need to be the captain and the head coach, to marshal resources and point the way.

Do you, as a leader, consider yourself organized or spontaneous? Are you able to plan ahead and "begin with the end in mind," or are you more inclined to wing it? Are you able to prioritize your time and put first things first, or do you take life as it comes? Do you plan to invest significant amounts of time in the Body Building process, or are you going to give it the leftovers? Your answers to these questions will significantly impact what you can expect from the Body Building series. Body Building is like a car that you can choose to drive 20 miles an hour or 70. You can use it to run errands around town or travel cross-country. How far it takes you will depend in no small degree on your ability to plan ahead carefully. **Whether you choose large goals or something more limited, you can be a success either way.** We offer a menu of possible outcomes so you can be successful within who you are. If organization is not your strong suit, you and your leadership can still achieve large goals if you take the time to incorporate people with the gift of administration into the process. There is wisdom in a multitude of counselors.

Church Condition: Some members' attitudes are so hardened that it would be real progress just to put a few cracks in the cement. Some churches are so allergic to change that it would be a wonderful achievement just to move them off dead center. On the other hand, there are churches that are revved up spiritually and ready to race ahead. Your church probably falls somewhere between a horse-and-buggy and a sports car. Success should be defined in relation to your own circumstances. It is not really fair to compare one church with another or expect the same results. **Success is defined by how well you cooperate with what the Spirit is currently trying to accomplish in your particular church**.

Note: If you anticipate having the Body Building Group continue in some form after this lesson series is over, you will need to give special attention to "Re-contracting" in Section V. 6 of this manual. (A helpful resource book on knowing your direction ahead of time is *The Purpose-Driven Church*, by Rick Warren.)

II. Preparation

1. Communicating with Leadership

Every congregation has **leaders** who are in voted positions and **influencers** who do not hold office but nonetheless exert persuasive power among the members. An eighty-year-old widow may exert far more influence behind the scenes than a much younger head elder. If you do not recognize this fact, you can be blindsided by unnecessary criticism and never get your new emphasis off the ground. Influencers can persuade *positively* and reinforce desired change, or they can persuade *negatively* and have veto power over change. One pastor thought he had smooth sailing after his head elder, head deacon, and Sabbath school superintendent all agreed privately with a new proposal. When it came time for the church board to decide, however, they all inexplicably voted against it. What happened? The pastor didn't realize that the head elder's wife actually had far more influence on certain people than he did, and she didn't like that new proposal one single bit. Open communication with key leaders and influencers is vital. You cannot be a lone ranger and be successful. Don't get too far ahead of your people. You do not need 100 percent support before you initiate change, but you do need to carefully and prayerfully assess whose support is critical.

As you seek to communicate what Body Building is about, avoid trying to give detailed explanations about what is in the lessons. Unless people have studied the lessons, you can create misunderstanding by trying to summarize and share too much at first. The essential thing to convey is your vision for what church can become. Explain that Body Building has the potential of helping the church accomplish that vision. Share one-on-one in leaders' homes first, then at the church board. Whether you feel you need the church board's permission or just need to inform them depends on your own situation.

Caution! Because the first Body Building Group is usually made up of leaders who join through personal invitation, others who are not invited can feel left out. The initial group could be labeled as a clique. To avoid this, tell the church board that these concepts are best understood in a small-group setting, and therefore you can only process a dozen or so people at a time. Assure them that you will be planning future groups if the experience is as helpful as you expect. You can inform the rest of the church by having members of the current Body Building Group give brief testimonies just prior to or during the church service. Have them tell the members that the first phase focuses on leadership training, and that it will eventually be made available to whomever is interested.

Don't raise the general membership's expectations too high at first. Let Body Building sell itself gradually. Word of mouth works best in generating interest. Try to create an *inclusive* attitude. Tell those who are not chosen for the beginning group, "I'm going to make all my mistakes on this group so I can get it right when we come to you." Later Body Building Groups can be made available through a general sign-up. You cannot avoid all misunderstanding, but you can keep it to a minimum.

2. When and Where to Meet

Because the Body Building Lessons take about four months to complete, you could plan to start in early September, to avoid as many holidays as possible, or in January, to avoid the vacation times of spring and summer. There have been, however, many successful Body Building Groups that started later in the fall and carried over well into the new year, taking breaks for holidays in between. Meetings typically run from 7:00 to 8:30 p.m. or 7:30 to 9:00 p.m. Be sure to be faithful to the time boundaries you set. The group may find it necessary to take a week off sometime because of vacations, church programming, or holidays, but **overall continuity is a must**. Don't make the meeting schedule sporadic. Once you set a night, stick with it. Tuesday or Wednesday evenings seem to work well.

We have also found it best to meet in someone's *home* rather than the church or school building. The home atmosphere is much more conducive to fellowship and openness. Every meeting night try to have someone at the door fifteen minutes ahead of time to greet group members warmly. Choose a host home and have the chairs arranged in a circle with no table in between. There is really no need to offer refreshments, except perhaps glasses of water nearby. Young children and pets should be cared for so there will be minimal interruption.

3. Whom to Invite

A typical Body Building Group will have eight to twelve members, including the pastor/leader.

    a. In order for this new vision to permeate your congregation, you will need to have as many as possible of your *key leaders* in the first groups to act as leaven in the church and give you support in future decision making. Start with the inner core and work out from there.

    b. Be sure to include both spouses in your invitation whenever possible. We have found that having only one spouse catch the vision of Body Building can be·frustrating to the other partner, who often feels left out.

    c. It can add spice to a group to get a mix of people: older/younger; single/couples; talkative/quiet; open/closed; longtime Adventist/new Adventist. A number of non-Adventists have also enjoyed the group experience. This mix can help group chemistry. One caution to keep in mind, however, is that the more divergent the ages, backgrounds, and theological perspectives of members, the more effort it may take to create a close bond of understanding and openness.

    d. Potential group members should not be pushing an extreme theological agenda.

    e. One good way to revive church members who are apathetic or on the verge of dropping out is to invite some of them to each group as well. The group dynamic can become infectious as they associate with more active, enthusiastic members. Pray earnestly about your selection.

f. One church has been very successful at taking time at the end
   of the Body Building Lessons to ask the current group itself
   who they think should be in the next group. They can then
   become instrumental in inviting those people themselves.

4. How to Invite People

Although it may initially seem daunting to ask people to join a small group
for 16 weeks, many other types of groups stay together for well over a
year. Tell them that you are trying to avoid the quick fixes that so often
fizzle out. You want to build deeply. Emphasize the vision and potential
for their church rather than the time period. Demonstrate an upbeat, *try
it, you'll like it* attitude. Read the lessons ahead of time so you can speak
from experience. People also need to hear what you think Body Building
can do for them personally. People are very busy and might be thinking,
What's in this for me? Is it really worth this much time? Make it clear that
the group experience can help *them* discover the oneness with fellow
Adventists that Jesus prayed for. It can also open new avenues for *their*
Christian experience to be much more fulfilling and enjoyable.

You should invite potential group members personally. Try to meet with
them in their home or in a quiet, unhurried situation so that you can share
some of the vision that burns within your own heart. **Don't try to tell a
lot about the lessons, just enough to capture their interest**. At this
point you are *not* asking them to actually join the Body Building Group.
All you are asking is that they come to an Exploration Meeting. The
Exploration Meeting introduces them to the concept of the Body Building
series in a group setting. (More will be said about the Exploration Meeting
in the next section.) People are more likely to respond positively in a
group setting than when they are alone. If they seem interested during
your home visit, ask them to pray earnestly about the upcoming
Exploration Meeting, inviting the Holy Spirit to do a special work in the
members' hearts.

When inviting people to the Exploration Meeting, your **enthusiasm will
mean more than your specific words**. Adventists are too used to

hearing a lot of information and glowing promises of great programs. Everything can seem important; therefore, nothing appears important. The best way they can sort out what really matters is by the leader's own level of enthusiasm. It is the look in the eye, the tone of voice, the sense of excitement that will convey far more than words at this stage. Thirty-eight percent of what is communicated comes from the speaker's tone inflection, emphasis, and energy. Fifty-five percent of your message comes from what the listeners see, such as gestures and movement. **Only seven percent of the message comes from what is heard, the words themselves** (*Why Nobody Learns Much of Anything at Church: And How To Fix It*, p. 191). In order to convey a sense of importance and urgency, you will have to bring that importance into your attitude, voice, and mannerisms. The greatest truth spoken with dullness will fall on deaf ears.

5. The Exploration Meeting

People come to this meeting to explore what the Body Building Series is all about. They should have a *come and see* attitude. This is an opportunity to learn and experience more before they decide whether or not to join. The goal is to heighten their awareness of the need to understand God's vision for church and to encourage them to sign on. You should have shared enough of your vision when you personally invited them that they have a high degree of interest already. The Exploration Meeting will last about ninety minutes, the same as a regular Body Building Group meeting. It should be held at the home of the person who will be the host for the rest of the series. Have the host/hostess greet the members warmly when they arrive. Make sure everyone is comfortable. Open with prayer.

At the Exploration Meeting you can do the following:

a. Group Activity or Ice Breaker

People will come to this meeting wondering what to expect. They may even be somewhat apprehensive. You can help put them at ease by opening with a fun activity. Please choose *one* of the following group activities or of the *one* of the Ice Breakers. (You may, of course, use one of your own.) Keep it light and upbeat. Choose something that fits the personality of your group.

Group Activities .

Me and My Hat

Bring different types of material to make hats, such as colored construction paper, newspapers, ribbon, bows, wrapping paper, plus scotch tape and scissors. Have each person make a hat. Tell them you are looking for creativity and innovation. Encourage people to use as many different materials as possible. After ten or fifteen minutes have a hat parade. Then each person should describe their hat and tell what they had in mind when they made it.

When all have finished, ask the group whether they saw a side of people they hadn't seen before. You can make the point that an important part of church is rejoicing in our creativity and the variety of ways God made us. We all contribute something unique. All are important, as illustrated by the fact that if just one hat had been missing, the group's joy would have been diminished. We are as different as our hats, yet we also hold much in common.

My Life Journey

You will need several types of popular magazines from newsstands or your own home that have a variety of pictures, plus a bottle of glue and pair of scissors for each person. Have them cut out pictures from the magazines to make a collage or mural that highlights various stages or aspects of their lives. They could focus on things the group may not know too much about, such as their interests and activities as a youth. They may also want to include something about their current hobbies or dreams for the future. If they can't find just the right picture, they can draw it. There should be no writing, only pictures. You can give each member a large brown shopping bag or some other material on which to paste their collage. Encourage creativity and innovation. After about fifteen minutes have each person show his or her production and explain. Make the application that we are all unique and important. Ask if they learned some new things about each other. (From *Building Community In Youth Groups*, by Denny Rydberg, p. 60, Group Books, Box 481, Loveland, CO 80539)

Gumdrop Tower

Divide into groups of three or four. As much as possible mix people with others they don't know well. Give each group gumdrops, wooden matches, and uncooked regular spaghetti noodles. (Have extra supplies.) Give them around 15 minutes to build a tower as high as they can. Use the gumdrops as connectors. All groups build at the same time. Each tower must be able to stand by itself. After the time is up you can declare a winner, then debrief by asking everyone some or all of the following questions:

- "How many different ideas did you consider in making your tower?"
- "What were the group members' roles in building the tower?"
- "In what ways did you function well as a group?"
- "What was frustrating about this activity?"

Then you can make this application: "How is this exercise like—or unlike—the way God wants us to function together as church?" (*Building Community In Youth Groups*, Denny Rydberg, p. 39)

Ice Breakers
- "Given one day to do anything I'd like, with no economic constraints, I would choose to. . . ." "One unfulfilled dream of mine is. . . ." (From *101 Best Small-Group Ideas*, by Deena Davis, p. 88, 89)

- "If there were 25 hours in a day, what would you add to your daily schedule?" "What was your first job?" (From *Ice-Breakers and Heart-Warmers*, by Steve Sheely, p. 50, 66)

- "What is one of your happiest memories from childhood and why?" "Describe your first car."

b. Your Testimony

As the leader you may now share something of your own spiritual journey as a church member, your hopes and frustrations, the hurts and dreams. Your sharing should not be a generalized history of your life as a Christian but ought to focus on how you have longed for yourself and the church members to become a growing, joyful, nurturing spiritual community. Tell them why you are hopeful now and how you feel the Body Building Group experience can make a real difference for the future of the church. Let them know how confident you are in the possibilities God has in store if only your church understands and follows the biblical principles in the Body Building Lessons. **Help them to feel like pioneers and adventurers**. Your own openness at the beginning can have a positive effect on group life later. This portion should last no more than 15 minutes. At the end of your testimony you could ask them,

- Was there anything in what I just shared that struck a cord in your own life?
- Have any of you ever felt like I have?
- How does what I've just said make you feel?
- Does anyone have something they'd like to share in response to what I have just said?

Their responses may take another 15 minutes.

c. Count the F's

This exercise can help sensitize the group to the fact that not everyone sees things the same way. It also highlights the fact that we need the collective wisdom of the group to understand all God has in mind for His people. (Make these applications only after the exercise is finished.)

Give out copies of the following paragraph. Pass it out face-down so the members cannot see what is written ahead of time. Ask them to keep it blank side up until you indicate. (See Appendix A for a full-page reproducible copy.)

Count The F's

> FEATURE FILMS ARE THE RE-
> SULT OF YEARS OF SCIENTI-
> FIC STUDY COMBINED WITH
> THE EXPERIENCE OF YEARS

Explain that you want them to read the paragraph through and count how many times the letter "F" is used. Tell them not to count the title but just the paragraph itself. When you say Go, they should be given only twelve to fifteen seconds before they stop and turn the papers over again. Ask how many found three occurrences of "F," then have them put down their hands. Next ask how many found four, then five, and finally six. The answer is six. Have them look at the paragraph again to find them all. People usually overlook the word "of." Now you can debrief by asking how those who counted three or four felt when they saw people raising their hands for five or six. How did those who counted five or six feel when they saw people respond with three? Was that unsettling in any way? Make it fun and lighthearted.

The point is that they all had the same paragraph and the same time period but saw different things. Could that also be true of God's revelation in Scripture? We all have the same Bible, but we don't all see everything that is there. That is why we need each other and this small group to help us understand God's purposes for His people.

d. Personal Belief Window

This exercise underscores the fact that we all see things differently and need each other to get a full picture. Introduce this exercise by saying, "Now let's look further at the idea that we need each other to understand God's plans and purposes." Get a common metal coat hanger (one that is wire all around, without plastic or cardboard). Turn it upside down and hold onto the hook, which is now on the bottom. Then grab the long straight piece of wire on top and pull upward in the middle until the coat hanger forms a diamond shape. This is now a Personal Belief Window.

(Hold it in front of your face and look through it during this explanation.) Tell people that everyone has one of these in front of his or her face all day, every day. It is invisible, but it is there. We view life through this window. Everything we see or hear passes through it. It acts like a filter. Everyone's window is different. Ask the group members what they think would make up a person's window. Our windows are made up of all our past experiences, education, upbringing, reading, values, culture, personality, etc. We do not so much see things in life as they are, but as we are. The window can distort. Ask the group how a person's Personal Belief Window can be changed. The Body Building Lessons are designed to help bring about that change.

e. Lessons & Format

Pass out the Body Building Lessons and go over the table of contents. Highlight three or four lesson themes that particularly capture your interest. Point out that the lessons are solidly based on Scripture and the Spirit of Prophecy. Have them turn to the first lesson, "What Is Church— Part A," and go over the lesson format. Underscore how the Reflection and Review Questions help us listen to and understand each other better. The Group Activities bond us together. The Love in Action segments help us grow through service. Emphasize that the more they put into the Body Building Group, the more they will get out of it. You do not actually study this lesson until next week. However, if you need to fill up the time, you can launch into the first couple of pages. Invite their input.

f. Guidelines and Covenant

Tell them this is not an ordinary group. This group can make a significant difference for the future of their church. Therefore, you are asking for a significant commitment on their part. Hand out copies of the Body Building Group Guidelines and review them carefully. Also give out copies of the Group Covenant and explain it carefully. (Both the Guidelines and Covenant appear in **Appendix A** at the end of the manual.) Tell the group you would like all members to sign the Covenant, as much for themselves as for the group. Some will want to hand it in that night. However, make sure to let them know that they don't need to hand it in until after the group studies the second lesson. This takes the pressure off and gives them an opportunity to see what they are actually getting into. Once they taste the Body Building Group experience, they will usually be more likely to commit. By the end of the second meeting, everyone who is going to continue should have given you the signed Covenant. Be sure to collect them. If people are genuinely interested but for some reason need more time to decide, respect their feelings as much as possible.

When you hand out the Body Building Group Guidelines and Covenant, let people know that even though you would love to have everyone join the group, it is perfectly acceptable not to join, and no questions will be asked. No one should be made to feel guilty for not joining. Because some may not sign up, it might be good to invite a few more than you eventually hope to have.

By the end of the second meeting a Body Building Group is usually closed to new people joining. This is to help the group develop a sense of community and commitment to each other. People should not pop in and out randomly. Anyone who wants to join after the second lesson can be told that they will be at the top of the list for the next group. Help people understand why they need to wait.

g. Family Needs and Prayer

At the end of the evening you should ask those with babysitting needs to stay after so you may personally assist them with meeting those needs. The group may want to have several couples team up to hire a babysitter who can come to the same home where the meetings are held and take care of the children in another room.

Finally, have a dedication prayer and sing a chorus together, holding hands around the circle.

III. The Group Experience

1. Group Leadership

The Body Building Group leader must give the group high priority. The members will only make the group as much of a priority as the leader does. The leader should clear the decks and focus on the following:

a. Learning how to lead a small group. Previous experience as a group leader is not a requirement for starting a Body Building Group, though it would certainly be helpful. The following are some excellent sources for materials on small-group leadership:

The Small-Group Leaders Training Course by Dr. Judy Hamlin
Navpress
PO Box 35001
Colorado Springs, Colorado 80935
1-800-366-7788

How to Lead Small Groups by Neal F. McBride
Navpress (same address as above)

North American Division Evangelism Institute (ask for catalog)
9047 U.S. 31 North, Suite 3
Berrien Springs, MI 49103
1-616-471-9220

Serendipity House (ask for catalogue)
PO Box 1012
Littleton, CO 80160
1-800-525-9563

   b. Personal recruitment of group members.

   c. Preparation time for each group meeting. Your preparation
should focus mainly on developing the skills of a group facilitator and
thinking about how to draw out the thoughts and feelings of the
members.

   **d. Spending one evening each week actually conducting the
group.** Make every effort to avoid breaking the continuity of meeting on
a weekly basis. And be on time.

   e. Making personal visits to group members. A caring visit may
be appropriate as a follow-up to a personal need expressed by a group
member. The leader should also visit every group member individually
halfway through the Body Building Group Lessons to see how they are
reacting to the lessons and group experience. This mid-course visitation
can reap rich dividends. Neglecting it can also allow little problems to
fester until people vote with their feet and either stop coming or drop out
of the process at the end. If someone misses a meeting, make sure a group
member contacts them by phone to let them know they are missed.

Even though your role as leader is certainly important, you should not feel
that the success of the group depends solely on you. The Holy Spirit is
the real Motivator and Sustainer in this process. Also, once the group
begins meeting, a certain momentum and energy will develop from within
the group itself. As one man has commented, "You can't learn how to
swim by correspondence. You've got to get in the water." Launch out in
faith, and the Lord will certainly bless.

2. Dynamics of a Body Building Group Meeting

a. Discussion

Let the group do most of the talking. Your role is similar to that of a
person playing a pin ball machine. Remember when you put in your 50
cents as a youngster and hit the ball with the flipper? The longer you
could keep the ball banging around between the posts, the higher your
score would be. Likewise, try to keep the lines of communication going

between the group members rather than always coming back to you. You may have to tell people to respond to others and not always back to you. When someone makes a comment to you, turn it back to the group by asking, "Who would like to respond to Frank's comment?" or "How do the rest of you feel about what Frank is saying?"

Initially you may have to spend some time in the role of teacher to get the ball rolling. Ideally the group itself will soon take on most of the teaching function. Draw out what the Holy Spirit is teaching them through the lesson material. Help them interact with and learn from one another. Their own thinking will deepen as various thoughts and feelings mingle. Members should expect to shape one another's ideas and experience.

Remember, discussion cannot be an end in itself. You could get an animated discussion going about politics or the death penalty, but that's not related to the lesson. The goal is meaningful discussion. If the group spends most of the evening debating church standards, you have probably missed the point.

Emory A. Griffen, in his excellent article, "The Greening of a Discussion Leader," offers several hints on how to generate meaningful discussion in a small group (*Leadership*, Winter Quarter, 1981, p. 103-115):

1. Ask yourself, "Do I really want a discussion?" The answer is not always "yes." Some group leaders inwardly love to teach and turn the small group into a kind of mini-classroom. Others are somewhat fearful of an animated discussion because they don't feel in control. They can also fear that some question might be asked that they can't answer or don't know how to handle.

2. It is a truism that "Communication = Content + Relationship." If you want people to open up, help them to feel safe and valued by getting to know them and building bonds of trust.

3. Don't ask questions that have only one right answer. You will not get much discussion by asking, "How many disciples did Jesus have?" If people are afraid they might give a wrong

answer, they will be quiet. But if there is room for a variety of answers and opinions, then they can jump in without fear. A better question might be, "How would you have felt if you were one of Jesus' disciples during the last week of His life?"

4. Encourage shy people to participate by making them the experts. Think ahead of time how you can tap into their experience and expertise to illustrate a point in the lesson. For instance, ask the homemakers how important it is to put all the ingredients in a recipe, to illustrate that we are all important to the church. Have they ever left something out of a recipe and what were the results? Or ask someone who is a mechanic about the different systems in a car and how they work together, to illustrate the way members need to work in harmony. Everyone is an expert on their own life, which can become a bridge to other areas of learning.

5. Monitor the environment. If the room is too small, too stuffy, too warm, or too cold, people's minds will be distracted. Provide everyone with comfortable seating.

6. Don't judge people's answers. Nothing will close people up faster than making them feel like they made a mistake. Be careful about labeling others as "wrong."

7. Don't preach. Small groups are a place for mutual discovery, not pontification about one's own agenda.

8. Plan ahead. As group leader, your most important task is to think through what discussion questions you are going to use. You may want to add to the ones already provided in the lessons themselves.

9. Use humor. Few things relax people more than laughter.

10. Don't be afraid of conflicting opinions. Don't try to smooth over all differences. It is OK for people to disagree, even strongly, as long as they don't put others down. An energized environment invites participation.

11. Seek balanced participation. "You need to deal head-on with the two thorniest problems facing a discussion leader: How to get the apathetic person to enter in and how to prevent the monopolizer from dominating the discussion. Both extremes spell trouble" (Emory Griffin).

The best way to get silent group members involved is to create an environment that is so interesting that they will burst if they don't get their two cents worth in. In dealing with domineering members, the firm approach often works best. You can say, "Kathy, you've put in some interesting ideas. Now give some others a chance." Sometimes you may have to interrupt a rambling monologue: "Hold it right there, Pete. You're tossing out a number of worthwhile ideas, but I'm not sure we can handle all of them at once. Take your first point, boil it down to one simple sentence, and we'll see what others think about it." You can also use affirmation, "Bill, you know a lot more about this than others in the group. I'm afraid your knowledge might intimidate them. How about hanging back a while so they can get in their licks without feeling stupid?" By doing this "you've deputized the monopolizer as an associate discussion leader, and he shares your concern to draw out others" (Emory Griffin).

If members have chronic personal needs, emotionally or spiritually, that dominate group life week after week, visit with them personally and help them find the assistance they need. Help them discover other outlets for their hurts so they won't overwhelm the group agenda on a regular basis.

12. One of the most effective means of getting people involved in the lesson material is to ask them to lead out in some or all of a certain night's meeting. You should provide coaching ahead of time and lots of affirmation. Not everyone is ready to take on the responsibility for an entire evening, but they may lead out in discussing a lesson parable, an illustration, or a reflection question.

13. Don't try to summarize what everyone said at the end of the meeting. You can review key points in the lesson, but if you try to summarize discussion you will inevitably make someone feel short-changed and misunderstood. It is OK to leave loose ends.

b. Presentation Methods

Various methods may be used in presenting the lessons. Don't start a group meeting by simply saying, "So, what did you think of the lesson this week?" Consider carefully the various possibilities below and use a **combination** that works best for you:

1. You may go through the lesson one page at a time. You may also divide it according to the different themes covered. Identify what you think are the main points of the lesson at home beforehand. At the meeting you will usually need to get the ball rolling by sharing how some point early in the lesson struck you and why. As soon as possible let the members jump in and express what impacted them. You can weave other points you identified ahead of time into the discussion as the evening unfolds. (Do not re-read large portions of the lesson at the meeting.)

2. Use the Reflection and Review Questions to provide a significant part of the focus for the evening.

3. Draw out some main points by focusing on the parables and illustrations. Most people think in concrete terms and can be most easily drawn into a discussion based on specific situations.

4. Don't be so concerned about "getting through the lesson" that you fail to pursue meaningful discussion. It is not easy to find the balance between breadth and depth, quantity and quality. Tell members you will conduct the meeting with the assumption that they have already read the lesson. Invite them to help make the evening a success by investing time in study and reflection.

Partway through the lesson series, it can be helpful to ask members how they feel about the approach you are taking to lesson presentation. You may want to get written feedback. It can also be enlightening to ask a couple group members with whom you feel very comfortable to confidentially share with you how they feel things are going.

c. Balancing learning and relationships

A Body Building Group's primary focus is on **learning**. You need to make sure that group members are actually studying and growing in their understanding and awareness. Try to cover what you and the group feel are the major points. Without this foundation of learning it will be difficult to make significant progress later on in changing church life.

However, it is also vital to allow significant time for developing supportive, caring **relationships.** The Body Building Lessons are presented in a small-group format so the members can actually experience the principles of caring presented in the lessons. For instance, many church members have never experienced genuine acceptance by others. That concept will come to life as they feel safe in sharing personal hurts and needs and have the group respond in a nonjudgmental way. Without the relational element, the group experience is sterile and remains just another mental exercise. **Don't ever allow the group experience to become a lecture.** As leader, you will have to decide what is the proper balance between learning and developing relationships on any given night. Look at the trend over several lessons rather than being too concerned if one night is imbalanced. In fact, there are some nights when the Spirit may want you to spend much more time than usual ministering to a soul in need. It is very helpful if you take time spontaneously during group meetings to pray briefly for personal needs that are expressed during the discussion and to sing choruses of rejoicing over good news. We want the members to experience true body life.

d. Five Communication Levels [see beginning of lesson "The Disciple's Heart"]

It is helpful when leading a small group to realize there are five levels of communication. Each level goes deeper in helping us understand and know the other person.

1. **Cliche**—This conversation is about the weather, etc. It is helpful in getting a conversation started, but is just friendly chit chat and does not reveal very much about the other person.

2. **Facts**—This is reporting facts about the family, job, house, friends, etc. For instance, "My little Johnny just joined the basketball team." "Our family is going to Yellowstone for a vacation this summer." "Martha was in a car accident yesterday." Again, this is a helpful part of communication, but we still don't know too much about the person.

3. **Ideas**—In this type of communication people share what they think about something. For instance, "I think they ought to lock drunk drivers away for thirty years, minimum." "I think we are living very near the end of time." "I don't think Adventists pray enough." Now we are getting to know people quite a bit better because we are learning something about their opinions.

4. **Feelings**—It is here that we really get a much better under-standing of what is going on inside people. They describe their feelings, from joy to anxiety.

   Suppose someone is telling you about her prospects for a new job. She begins by saying, "I'm applying for a new job." That is fact. Then she continues, "I think it would be a good challenge for me." That is idea or opinion. So far we know a little bit about her. But suppose she then goes on to say, "You know what, I'm scared stiff about that interview." That's feeling. Now we can really empathize with her and provide caring and support because we know her so much better on the inside.

5. **Intimate Sharing**—Here people share their innermost dreams

and needs. This kind of sharing is usually reserved for marriage or very close friendships. If it occurs during group life, it needs to be valued and handled with tenderness and care.

As you become aware of the five levels of communication, you will quickly recognize that most conversation doesn't go much below level three. Sabbath school classes usually spend most of their time on levels one, two, and three. It takes skill on the part of the group facilitator to guide a group into level four communication. Sharing on level three— **ideas**—enables the group to focus on learning. Sharing on level four— **feelings**—helps the group focus more on support and love. Feeling is also an important part of learning as you discover people's attitudes toward both the material they are studying and the group process itself. They may agree that something is factual but not feel committed to it at all.

You cannot and should not force someone to share on levels four and five. However, you can provide opportunities and open the door by modeling that kind of openness yourself. Also, consider the types of questions you ask. Do they start with "What do you think . . ." or with "How do you feel about . . ."? During a Body Building Group meeting, try to guide the conversation through the first four levels. **Group communications should fluctuate between levels**. It is not good to spend too much time on level one or two. On the other hand, if a group spends most of its time on level four, the evening may seem too intense and intimidating for some members, especially at first. The important point is to be aware of how communication is flowing between the levels and how effective that flow is. You are the gatekeeper and guide.

e. Prayer

One of the best ideas I have found for Body Building Group prayer is a Prayer Pouch. Have someone make a cloth pouch about 8 inches wide by 6 inches deep, with a cloth flap. At some point in the evening discuss prayer needs and answers to prayer. Write needs down on 3x5 cards and put them in the pouch. Have a member of the group (or a couple) volunteer to take the pouch home that week and pray over the needs each day. Next week the pouch is rotated to another member. Take out the cards of answered prayers and insert new ones. Vary the prayer experiences in the group.

f.　Timing

Start and end on time. Don't wait until everyone is there before you start. By waiting you penalize those who made the effort to be on time. Don't serve refreshments; it only delays starting and makes future hostesses feel they must entertain. The best time to shut down a group for the evening is when everyone is saying, "Oh, we can't stop now!" That will guarantee they will be back next week to pick up where they left off. If people have more questions or comments to share, you should close the meeting on time with the announcement that anyone who wants to stay after is welcome to do so.

g.　Evaluations

Evaluations can be a very helpful part of the Body Building experience. Some leaders have had their group members fill out an evaluation survey about halfway through the lessons and then another at the end. If we only evaluate at the end, the current group cannot benefit. Simply hand out blank pieces of paper and have group members answer three questions, without putting their names on the papers:

1. How do you feel so far about the content of the lessons?
2. What do you like best about the group experience and how can it be improved?
3. What does the group leader do well, and what can he/she improve?

You may prefer to make up your own questions. For the mid-course evaluation, look over the papers during the week. When the group meets again, assure them that you have read all the evaluations carefully. It can be helpful to report back to the group some of the points that affect everyone. These evaluations let the group know you take Body Building seriously. If evaluations make you nervous, just do one when you finish.

h. Retreats

Body Building Groups should normally hold a retreat one or two weeks after the lesson series is finished. The retreat can be in someone's home and last from two to four hours. **The key is to also invite members of all the previous Body Building Groups your church has held**. This provides continuity and builds momentum and a sense of community. At the retreat you can eat, sing songs, pray, do ice breakers, share testimonies about Body Building Group experiences, do group activities, talk about visions for the future, lay plans for future Body Building Groups, etc. An excellent resource for your retreat is the video "Turning Vision Into Action" by George Barna. It will spark fruitful discussion on how to take the vision you have been studying in these lessons and make it a reality in your church. The video lasts about forty minutes and can be ordered by calling 1-800-55-BARNA. You may also contact The Barna Research Group, LTD, in Oxnard, California.

3. Special Features

Just because you put eight to twelve people together in a room for 16 weeks does not guarantee that they will become an effective group. A healthy group contains the three key elements of (1) learning, (2) mutual support, and (3) ministry to others outside the group. A healthy group is a safe place with interaction and communication on various levels. Too many people are used to sitting in a Sabbath school class or seminar and simply discussing ideas. They do not share on a heart level or commit to acting on what they learn.

The small-group experience with these lessons is not supposed to be just one more class. In order to help remodel people's understanding of what group life can be, the lessons contain Special Features in addition to the

lesson material itself. It is vital that you, as the leader, take these very seriously. The lesson material is central and will occupy most of the meeting
time. The Special Features are designed to enhance the group experience
and help make the principles contained in the lesson a reality.

The Special Features are described in general below. The particular
Special Features contained in each lesson will be described more fully in
Section IV of the manual.

a. Learning to be a Group

People need to be taught group skills. At the beginning of each lesson is
a brief section on some aspect of how to be an effective group. This
provides your members with a 16-week mini-course. You should call the
members' attention to this section each week before you start studying
that particular lesson. You may ask them how that principle would impact
group life and how they think the group has been applying it so far. You
can review them with the group periodically.

b. Love in Action Feedback

This is an opportunity for group members to give feedback on the Love
in Action ministry suggestion at the end of the previous lesson. A more
complete explanation of this feature is given in this section under letter
"g."

c. Ice Breakers

During the first few meetings you will have to pay special attention to
what is called "group building." **Take time to build trust and openness**.
The chemistry of the group has to be developed. Until that happens the
discussion of the lessons themselves can easily remain stilted. People only
speak from their hearts when they feel they are in a safe atmosphere. Ice
Breakers can be an invaluable way of helping create that atmosphere.

Read the Ice Breaker for that week and have people react. During the first few sessions you may have to give the first response. Your own candor and honesty will model for the group the way you hope they will share. Don't be afraid of silences; give people time to reflect and participate.

Ice Breakers need not always be done with the entire group together. Especially at first, you can overcome people's nervousness by doing the Ice Breakers in "breakout groups" of two, three, or four people. You may then have each breakout group briefly share some of their answers. There are various ways to divide into breakout groups:

- Count off around the circle by three's or four's (all 1's form a group, all 2's form a group, etc).
- Select three or four group leaders at random and let the people join the group they wish. All groups must be the same size.
- Have them spontaneously form groups of two or three with people they have not been in a breakout group with before. No leaders assigned.
- Have group members line up according to the date of their birthdays (not the year!). Then divide up by two's, three's, or four's from left to right.
- Put the same number of colored M&M candies in a bowl as there are members of the group. If you want groups of three, put in three red M&Ms, three greens, etc. Mix up the M&Ms and have the members take one without looking. All reds in a group, etc.
- Be creative!

Most of the time Ice Breakers should be done with the whole group in one circle. An Ice Breaker usually doesn't take more than 10 to 15 minutes. Don't let it drag. People should not feel pressured or compelled to share. It is usually better to simply ask who would like to share an answer rather than going around to each person in turn, which can be rather intimating to some people.

A good source for other Ice Breaker questions is the book, *201 Great Questions* by Jerry D. Jones, Navpress, PO Box 35001, Colorado Springs,

CO 80935, 1-800-366-7788.

d. Group Activity

This is another method for group building. These activities involve the entire group in a brief exercise that illustrates some part of that evening's lesson. Far from being entertainment, such group activities are valuable for various reasons:

1. They tend to draw the group together in nonthreatening ways.
2. They provide a different method of learning. This can appeal especially to group members who learn best by seeing and doing.
3. They encourage an atmosphere of adventure and discovery.
4. They provide a helpful break from what can be a rather intense evening.

Explain this value to the group. Most activities should not take more than 15-20 minutes. Be flexible, but don't let it eat into lesson time. Be sure to debrief after the activity to see what people learned. **You don't have to do a Group Activity at the beginning of the evening.** It can be very effective to do the Group Activity at some other point in the lesson time to provide variety. Don't be entirely predictable.

e. Reflection Questions

At various points throughout each lesson are Reflection Questions. These are designed to highlight aspects of the lesson material and help the group wrestle with concepts.

f.   Review Questions

At the end of each lesson are Review Questions that serve as a wrap-up, again highlighting key points. You do not have to use all the questions in each lesson. Feel free to make up your own discussion questions.

g. Love in Action

Whenever you see a Love in Action Feedback at the beginning of a lesson, it is referring back to the Love in Action ministry that was described on the last page of the previous lesson. The purpose of Love in Action is to help group members become more outward-focused in ministry. This is a critical aspect of breaking up Laodicean attitudes and developing healthy group life. The temptation will be very strong to ignore the Love in Action. Don't give in to that temptation. When you have finished discussing one of the lessons at your group meeting, take 5-10 minutes to read the Love in Action on the last page. That particular ministry is to be carried out during the next week. (Some Love in Action ministries take two weeks, such as collecting money for a present and making a fruit basket.) You always have two choices for ministry. "My Choice" is a suggestion from the lesson author. "Your Choice" is an opportunity for the group to think up an alternative.

At the beginning of the following week's lesson there is the Love in Action Feedback, which gives the members a chance to reflect on how they did with the previous week's ministry suggestion. It provides some account-ability as well. In soliciting feedback, don't go around to each person in the group. Just open it up for sharing time. When group members report, celebrate little efforts to reach out. Offer a prayer of thanks at the end asking God to take these simple efforts and multiply them through His Spirit. Don't make this time oppressive or guilt-producing. Above all, keep it upbeat and encouraging. If your group members do not do the Love in Action ministry, don't press the issue. You will need to lead by doing the ministries yourself. **Let your example and testimony be an encouragement**. You can also ask one or two members to do the ministry with you to get the ball rolling.

When people report on their activities, let them know they were doing real ministry and were fulfilling their role as God's priests. Throughout the series, keep reinforcing the concept that they are ministers for God.

The Lord has given us one of the great secrets to spiritual health in Isaiah 58:6-9: "Is this not the fast that I have chosen, to loose the bonds of wickedness, to undo the heavy burdens. . . . Is it not to share your bread with the hungry. . . . Then your light shall break forth like the morning, your healing shall spring forth speedily. . . . Then you shall call and the Lord will answer; You shall cry and He will say, 'Here I am.'"

One of the best ways to keep our own souls alive and to reinvigorate discouraged souls is to be disinterestedly sharing Christ's love in every way possible. Refuse to let the 16 weeks of small-group meetings be a time of taking without also giving and sharing outside the group.

IV. Explanation of Each Lesson

This section of the manual reproduces the following Special Features from each of the lessons and lists them according to the lesson in which they appear:

- Learning to be a Group
- Love in Action Feedback
- Ice Breakers
- Group Activity
- Love in Action

The purpose of this section is to provide further explanations for a number of these Special Features beyond what is in the lessons themselves. **Material that is reproduced here from the lessons is in italics. Additional comments are in normal type.**

It is important that you read through the explanations in this part of the manual for each lesson before conducting that particular small-group meeting. Leadership tips are also included.

If someone else is teaching all or part of a lesson, be sure to provide them with the material they will need from this section of the manual.

1. Lesson: What is Church—Part A

Special Features

Learning to be a Group

"A gathering of eight to twelve people does not [necessarily] constitute a group. A true group consists of a certain number of people who have committed themselves to one another and to a common goal. In essence they have agreed to struggle together. . . and care for one another." (Growth Through Groups, *William Clemmons & Harvey Hester, p. 111)*

Pay attention to educating the group members on how to be a group. Don't take it for granted that they understand. They will get far more out of the lesson material if the group life becomes a living example of the lessons themselves. In order for your group to be effective, it will take some very intentional educating and modeling on the part of the leader. Healthy group life depends on mutual commitment to the group and investment in its success. It also requires a certain degree of openness and willingness to be "church" to each other in new ways.

Ice Breaker

Describe one of your best friends from your elementary school years. What did you enjoy doing together the most?

Because this is the first meeting, try to keep the Ice Breaker as light and nonthreatening as possible.

Group Activity

Remodeling a Paper Cup.

The purpose of this activity is to help group members begin to explore their personal vision for church. Give each person a regular-size paper cup (not styrofoam). Ask them to picture in their minds the ideal church, what they always wished church could be. Then ask them to remodel the cup in a way that captures the essence of their vision. Here are some examples:

- Tear open the top to illustrate letting the Holy Spirit in.
- Make lots of doors to symbolize a welcoming, accepting atmosphere.
- Make lots of windows so the members can see out and not become self-absorbed.
- Cut several slits up from the bottom so that the church is flexible.
- Cut the cup into many pieces and scatter them in the world.

(Share one or two of these suggestions ahead of time as thought-starters). Tell them there are no right or wrong answers. You are looking for fun and creativity. Sometimes people cannot seem to get started on their own or are shy. Be watchful for this and help them out or team people up. After 10 to 15 minutes, ask them to share what their design is and what it symbolizes (don't go around the circle because that can make some people nervous). Be sure to praise their innovation and affirm their vision. Tell them that the Body Building Lessons are designed to build on and expand their dreams for church. **Most importantly the series will look at God's vision for church**. If some members are taking a long time to finish their cups, don't let the exercise drag on their behalf. You should supply all the cups, scissors, scotch tape, etc. You could also bring colored construction paper for added flare.

Love in Action (at end of lesson)
Sit by some lonely person in church this week and help him or her feel like an important part of God's flock.

The emphasis, or lack of it, that you put on the Love in Action ministry tonight can set the pace for the ministry opportunities in upcoming lessons. Don't rush or overlook this segment. As group leader, be sure to model this ministry yourself in order to report next week. If you are the pastor and have to preach on Sabbath, you could model this Love in Action step by sitting by a lonely person at church potluck or by going out of your way to speak to a lonely person after the worship service.

Leadership Tips

Don't rush into the meetings at the last minute. Make sure everyone who comes to the meeting receives a warm greeting when entering the house. Do everything possible to make members feel comfortable and tuned-in to what is happening. If any members arrive late, take time to greet them warmly, get them seats, and let them know where you are in the lesson.

All people are experts on their own experience. Try to draw out stories from group members relating to the three key words in this lesson—bride, living stones, and flock. Are there any interesting wedding stories group members have had? Perhaps someone who is a builder could talk about stone work and how it is done. Has anyone ever lived on a farm that had sheep?

At the end of this meeting, remind those who have not yet turned in their Group Covenant that you encourage them to do so by the end of the next meeting. If someone is still undecided at that time, they should not be excluded, but you could speak with them personally and see what they are feeling. Don't make such a big issue out of the Covenant that you exclude someone who really wants to come consistently but for some reason is not willing to sign.

Remember that people often come to the group meetings from very hectic days. The opening few minutes should help them unwind and get their heads and hearts focused on the meeting. That is one reason the Ice Breakers and Group Activities are so important. Singing a chorus can help also.

2. Lesson: What is Church—Part B

Special Features

Learning to be a Group

"Active listening" means giving people your full attention while they are talking and making an effort to listen for the meaning and feeling behind their words. Concentrate on what they are saying rather than simply

waiting for a chance to share your own thoughts.

The best way to teach good listening skills is to model them yourself. Try to look at people when they are talking. Don't be so intent on your own agenda that you fail to listen well.

Love in Action Feedback
Did you find a lonely person in church last Sabbath to encourage?

As people share their experiences, be sure to start reinforcing the idea that they are ministers for Christ. This concept is covered more fully in the lesson, "You Are A Minister!"

Ice Breaker
In what direction of the compass—north, south, east ,or west—have you traveled the farthest? What experience was the most enjoyable and/or most memorable?

Group Activity
What does your local church currently do very well?
Where could your church improve the most?

Church members will often be more open to change if at the outset of a Body Building Group you identify and affirm what their church does well. This Group Activity also gives them an opportunity to look at what needs to be improved. Put two large pieces of blank paper (easel-size) on the floor. Label one "Do Very Well" and the other "Improve." Take the two categories one at a time, writing down each suggestion in summary form. Write big enough for all to see. Be careful on the "Improve" list to let them know that they need to be sensitive to the feelings of group members. Have prayer over the lists, giving thanks and inviting the Spirit to help the church become all God wants it to be. Save the papers. At the end of the Body Building Lessons you can go back and review these lists and see if the members would make any changes.

Love in Action (at end of lesson)
Think of three people outside your group to whom you'd like to send an Encouragement/Appreciation Card. Each card would contain words of support and/or an expression of thankfulness for something they have done.

Once again, be sure to model the Love in Action portions of each lesson. It is very tempting to overlook these ministry opportunities, but the group will have a deeper experience if they take time to give of themselves outside the group.

Leadership Tips

Emphasize how important it is to study the lesson ahead of time. They can study a couple pages each day or reserve a larger portion of time on Sabbath. You might invite people to "buddy up" to hold each other accountable for studying if they wish. Any accountability should be voluntary, and no one should feel pressured.

Please Note: At the end of tonight's meeting, call attention to next week's Ice Breaker. It asks them to bring something from home for "Show and Tell."

3. Lesson: You are a Minister!

Special Features

Learning to be a Group

Participate, don't dominate. It is helpful not to talk too much or too little. Monitor yourself. Help people who are more shy and reserved to feel comfortable sharing. Strive for equality of input. Also, take time to read the lesson carefully ahead of time rather than cramming at the last minute. You will get out of the group what you put in.

Love in Action Feedback
Share something about your Encouragement/Appreciation Cards.

Ice Breaker
Please read this before the upcoming meeting! *We're going to do Show and Tell. Bring something this week from your home to show the group (other than a photo). Choose something that has special meaning for you.*

This simple activity can be the launching pad for people to spontaneously talk about aspects of their lives that are very meaningful but seldom heard. Be sensitive to underlying feelings that can help group members understand and appreciate each other more.

Group Activity: None this week.

Love in Action: (at end of lesson)
Give three hugs every day this week.

4. Lesson: Hey, Pastor!

Special Features

Learning to be a Group
It is better to speak for yourself, not others. Use words like "I" and "me" rather than "you" and "we." Also, go easy on the "oughts" and "shoulds."

It is best for each person to speak from their own perspective rather than assuming they know what others need to think or do. Frequent use of "ought" and "should" can impose unnecessary guilt feelings on other group members.

Love in Action Feedback
How did the Hug-A-Thon go this past week?

Ice Breaker
Guess Who?

Give each person in the group a blank 3x5 card. They should not put their names on them. Have them number the cards vertically on the left side, 1 through 5. They should then answer each of the following five questions. Tell them their answers are five clues about their identity. Each question begins with the phrase, "If I had to describe myself as a. . . ." (They don't write that phrase, just the answer.)

1. kind of animal
2. song or piece of music (give title)
3. type of food
4. place on earth
5. television program

Read the first question and have everyone write down an answer. Then read questions two, three, etc. When finished, put all the cards in a bowl and mix them up. The group leader picks them out one at a time. The leader then reads all the answers for one card and has the group guess verbally who it is. After all the guesses are in for that card, have the person reveal themselves and explain. Go on to the next card. (*Serendipity Youth Ministry Encyclopedia*, by Lyman Coleman, p. 61)

Group Activity: None this week.

Love in Action: (at end of lesson)
Put your loose change in a jar every day for a week and bring the jar to the next group meeting when you study "High-Rise Christians." At that meeting assign two members to think of a present they can buy for a person who is hurting.

5. Lesson: High-Rise Christians

Special Features

Learning to be a Group
Effective groups focus not only on learning, but also on building relation-ships. How we treat each other as we learn is as important as the learning itself. Effective groups also serve others. Ice Breakers, Group Activities, and Love in Action are important because they help bring balance to group life.

Love in Action Feedback
Time to put all the jar money into one pile. Assign two people to buy a present and deliver it this week to someone who is hurting.

One group had such fun with this activity that they decided to do it more than once during their time together. It can be especially effective if you give the present to a non-Adventist neighbor or friend. Let the group discuss possibilities and decide together. Explain the need to report back next week.

Ice Breaker: None this week.

Group Activity
Know Your String Bean.

The purpose of this game is to help group members see that each of us is unique. Buy enough fresh, whole, green string beans so that each person in your group will get one. (Keep a few extras in reserve). Select beans that look similar, have the same length, shape, etc. Give one bean to each group member. Tell them to give their bean a name and then become well-acquainted with their bean, study it, and learn all there is to know about their bean. After three or four minutes, collect all of the beans in a pan or hat. **Don't tell them why you are collecting them.** Mix all of the beans up and dump them in a pile on a table. Then ask the group members to find their beans. It is amazing how well they are able to do this. When then go back to their seats, ask if they are sure they found their bean. Then ask them to introduce the group to their bean and tell why they feel so sure that they found the right one. After the sharing, emphasize how all the beans looked alike at first, but as we got to know them better, we discovered that each one is unique. The point here is that God does not see crowds, only individuals, and because He knows us so well, we are unique and special to Him. We may each feel, "Oh, I'm just one of the church members." But actually we differ from everyone else in valuable ways. Everyone is needed.

Love in Action: None this week.

6. Lesson: The Joy of Gifts

Special Features

Learning to be a Group
Be sure to begin and end the meeting on time, except for unusual circumstances. Those who want to share further can be invited to stay by afterwards.

Love in Action Feedback
How did the purchase and delivery of the present work out?

Ice Breaker
What is one of the most memorable gifts you ever received? Why did it mean so much?

Group Activity: None this week.

Love in Action
Make a list of five things from the Bible and/or Spirit of Prophecy about how important you are to God. Paste that list in a place where you can see it every day for a week.

It would be helpful if you could do this exercise yourself ahead of time and read a couple of your quotes to give the group an idea of what to look for.

Important Notice

Have a group potluck next week on the same night you study "Opening Your Gifts." Come one hour early. You may only bring foods that begin with the letter "S."

You may either plan the potluck carefully and assign people entrees, desserts, etc. Or it can be fun to be spontaneous and see what turns up. Be sure to allow enough time for people to get there from work and still have about an hour for the potluck itself before the lesson study.

Leadership Tips

Please Note: Be aware of the following special activities that will take place during the three lessons on spiritual gifts. The two main elements are filling out the Johnson/Hunt Spiritual Gifts Questionnaire and Gift Giving. The full sequence of events is given here so you will know what to anticipate:

1. For the lesson "The Joy of Gifts"—When the group finishes studying this week's lesson, give out the Johnson/Hunt Spiritual Gifts Questionnaire. Explain how to fill out the questionnaire and scoring sheet. Ask the members to take it home, do the test, and score it themselves, then bring it to next week's meeting when you study "Opening Your Gifts." Explain that the Johnson/Hunt Questionnaire does not test for all the gifts listed in these lessons. The gifts of Healing, Craftsmanship, Music, and Prophecy are not on the questionnaire. They are certainly as important as any other gift, but it is felt that these four are best identified by means other than a question-and-answer test.

2. For lesson "Opening Your Gifts"—On the evening the group studies the lesson entitled "Opening Your Gifts," ask if there were any questions regarding the Johnson/Hunt Questionnaire. Members can then share their results.

At the end of that same evening you should pick names for Gift Giving. Gift Giving can be one of the most affirming and uplifting activities of the entire lesson series. Take the time to do this with care. The purpose is to affirm people's spiritual gifts and abilities.

At the end of the meeting pass out a blank piece of paper to each of the members. Have them put their names on their papers. Collect the papers and put them in a bowl. Each member should draw a name, making sure that no one gets his or her own name or that of a spouse. Have them purchase a gift for that person for under $2 (or whatever you decide) to bring to next week's meeting. Tell them not to forget! As leader you should bring gifts for members who were not present at that night's meeting. Tell the members that the gift should symbolize and affirm either one of the spiritual gifts they see in that person or some other ability. They can also affirm some way the person has been an asset and blessing to the group itself.

3. For lesson "Gift Wrap"—The gifts should be given out on the same night you study "Gift Wrap." It is usually done at the beginning of the meeting. Make sure everyone gets a gift. Don't let this drag on, but be sure to allow enough time for everyone to feel affirmed. Each member presents a gift and tells what it means, while the others watch. You may announce at the beginning that any of the other group members should feel free to add their own verbal affirmations in addition to what the person who presents the gift says. This can be a great time to tap into the energy and insight of the group as they attempt to help other group members discover their God-given spiritual gifts and abilities. Overall it should take 25-30 minutes. Finish by celebrating these affirmations in a prayer circle and singing a simple chorus.

7. Lesson: Opening Your Gifts

Special Features

Did you eat too much at the group potluck tonight?!

Learning to be a Group

Your group will get much more out of its time together if each person commits to specifically praying for the other group members during the week. At group meetings you can also help each other stay on the lesson topic during discussion as much as possible. And remember, confidentiality is a must.

It can be helpful to voluntarily set up prayer partners of two or three people toward the beginning of the group experience. Prayer will definitely be one of the keys to success. When you pray within the group itself, vary the experience. For example, some nights focus on praise for who God is or on specific aspects of Jesus' life. Other nights thank Him for specific evidences of our worth. You may also invite people to share how group prayer could help them right now in their own Christian experience: "Would anyone like to share some struggle they are experiencing that we can pray for?" Be creative and uplifting. Make group life a safe haven of encouragement. Also, don't forget the Prayer Pouch described in section III.2.e of this manual.

Love in Action Feedback

Did that list of five ways you are important to God help get you through the week?

Ice Breaker

What is one of the riskiest things you have ever done? How did it turn out?

Group Activity: None this week.

Love in Action: None this week.

Important Notice

After studying this lesson together, the group should take time to pick members' names out of a hat before you head home. Then, during this week, think about one of the spiritual gifts you feel that person has. (Phone the group leader if you are unsure.) Purchase a small gift for the person, for not more than two dollars, that in some way symbolizes that spiritual gift. Bring it to the upcoming meeting when you study "Gift Wrap." At that meeting, time will be provided at the beginning to go around the circle, one by one, to give the gifts and explanations.

Refer back to Leadership Tips at the end of the previous lesson for detailed information on this Gift Giving activity.

8. Lesson: Gift Wrap

Special Features

Learning to be a Group
Effective groups pay attention to the "climate" during the meetings. Does the meeting feel warm and inviting or kind of cool and reserved? Is it accepting or judgmental? Trusting or cautious? People grow best in an atmosphere that is safe.

It can be helpful to reinforce these concepts throughout the series. Try to catch people doing something right. Whenever you see someone manifest the warm, nonjudgmental behavior you desire, call attention to it and highlight it. Explain why it is important. Modeling is a powerful teacher and can also be very affirming to the person you catch "doing it right."

Ice Breaker: None this week.

Group Activity:
Give each group member a small gift that symbolizes one of that person's spiritual gifts.

Refer back to Leadership Tips at the end of the lesson, "The Joy of Gifts," for detailed information on this Gift Giving activity.

Love in Action
Have the entire group think up some project they can do together during the next week or two to benefit someone in need. The project should last no more than a couple of hours. Sunday mornings are usually good. You might rake an elderly person's leaves, paint a fence, clean out gutters, wash windows, etc.

This ministry will undoubtedly take extra time and planning to set up, but it is well-worth the effort. One pastor recently told me about how a simple yard clean-up on a Sunday morning brought the group together in new ways and added greatly to their joy. If you want your members to be more outreach-oriented, it can happen through these relatively small deeds of kindness.

Leadership Tips
Don't forget to visit with members personally at the halfway point in the series. This visit should be more than a passing comment in the church foyer. See them in their home or at some other unhurried time at church or during the week. Let the group know ahead of time that you want to make these visits so no one feels singled out. There are several important issues that can be explored:

1. How they feel about the group experience. Is it meeting their needs? Is it living up to their expectations?
2. How they feel about the lesson material so far.
3. Are there any other things they would like to share?
4. Is there anything in your leadership style that could be improved?

Sometimes little things occur in group life that raise hidden concerns. These can get in the way of further growth and full participation. This visit is the time to understand what those concerns may be. This can also be a great time to see what help they may need in discovering their spiritual gifts and ministry. Be sure also to reaffirm how much you value their presence in the group. Try to think of some specific comment they made in the group or some specific thing they did that you can thank them for. Encourage them to keep coming. Let them know that you realize it is a significant commitment of time and that they are not taken for granted.

9. Lesson: The Orchestra

Special Features

Learning to be a Group
Be slow to give advice and counsel on how others should deal with their problems. Be sure you have listened well and remember that you cannot fully appreciate someone else's struggles until you've walked a while in their shoes.

Love in Action Feedback
Did you find a group project to do together yet?

Ice Breaker: None this week.

Group Activity
The Blind Circle.

The purpose of this activity is to illustrate how the body of Christ works. (The activity goes well with the parable of the orchestra in the lesson itself.) Push back chairs and tables so the group members can stand to form a circle and join hands. The number of people in the circle must be a multiple of four (such as eight or twelve). You need at least eight to make the activity work, and twelve is preferable. Leftover people can be observers and help enforce the rules. Once the circle is formed, tell the members to hang on tightly to their neighbors' hands and to close their eyes completely. They must keep their eyes closed until you say to open them. Now tell them that they have ten minutes to form a perfect square.

They can talk to each other but they cannot look or let go of hands. No leader should be appointed ahead of time. Tell them to let you know when the group feels, as a whole, that they are done. Then they open their eyes. If the group needs more than ten minutes, add a couple of minutes and a countdown for excitement.

When finished, go back to your original chairs and debrief the activity. Ask what they learned about how the body of Christ should function. Some key points to cover are:

1. How well did leadership function?
2. How well did people communicate?
3. Note how important it was that they all had a common mental picture of what a square looked like. If they had never seen a square, it would be impossible to form one together. Likewise, unless they share a common vision of what church should be, it would be just as impossible to form one together. In fact, the main purpose of the Body Building Lessons is to instill that mutual vision.
4. How well did they cooperate?
5. How did it feel to be part of the group?

Love in Action
Choose a church member who seems to feel outside the Fellowship Circle of your church. Do something this week to help the person feel more included.

10. Lesson: The Kiss

Special Features

Learning to be a Group
There are various roles that different people can play in a group—Encourager, Tension Reliever, Communication Helper, Harmonizer, Summarizer, Information Giver, Information Seeker, Hospitality Giver, Trust Builder, Process Observer, Reminder, Schedule Keeper, to name a few.

(see Joining Together, *David W. Johnson & Frank P. Johnson, p. 26, 27)*

This Learning to be a Group section provides a great opportunity to explore how the members use their spiritual gifts and other abilities to minister within the group. Several group roles or functions are listed in this section. Ask the group to discuss those roles in the light of one another's talents and gifts. It may be helpful to give each member a copy of the master list of group members' spiritual gifts and ask them how they see those gifts operating within the group roles mentioned above or in other ways. Affirm the importance of people's investment in group life. Try to find something to affirm about everyone.

Love in Action Feedback
Were you able to help someone move closer to the Fellowship Circle of your church?

Ice Breaker
What has been one of your more humorous or embarrassing moments in life?

Group Activity: None this week.

Love in Action
Phone a friend or family member that you haven't called in quite a while and express your appreciation for him or her.

Be sure to model doing this yourself and report next week. Don't be afraid to venture out and be vulnerable.

Leadership Tips
This is a good time to remind group members to be missionaries to their own church. (See section V. 3 of the manual.) Other church members will gauge the value of the group by the response of people who are already in it. Encourage group members to reach out to other church members with increased acceptance, kindness, affirmation, and love.

11.   Lesson: The Disciple's Heart

Special Features

Learning to be a Group
There are four levels of communication that are important to group life.
>   *Level 1: Cliches— "How is the weather?"*
>   *Level 2: Reporting Facts— "My car broke down this week."*
>   *Level 3: Ideas— "I really think small groups are important."*
>   *Level 4: Feelings— "I feel discouraged today."*
All levels are valuable, but we get to know and understand each other best on levels three and four.

During the group experience you can affirm people who make the effort to communicate on level four especially. Again, try to catch people doing something right. Highlight the behaviors you want to instill.

Love in Action Feedback
How did the friend or family member react to your phone call?

Ice Breaker
"You are invisible for one day, what will you do?" (Ice Breakers and Heart Warmers, *Steve Sheely, p. 56)*

Group Activity: None this week.

Love in Action
Bring fruit to the next group meeting when you study "The Telescope." Someone should also bring a basket to make a group fruit basket. Have a group member take it to a shut-in or homeless shelter after the meeting.

One small group planned on giving their fruit basket to a shut-in who was a member of their church. The person who was supposed to make the delivery forgot all about it, however, until late on the day of the group meeting. She didn't have time to run across town to the nursing home, so she decided to give the basket to a non-Adventist neighbor whose wife had recently died. The next day the person who gave the basket found it returned on her own doorstep with all the fruit gone. It was now filled with small gifts and included a note of deep appreciation from the neighbor. What a joyful report that church member gave at the next small-group meeting.

12. Lesson: The Telescope

Special Features

Learning to be a Group
It is helpful to keep the conversation on the subject at hand rather than taking too many sidetracks and "chasing too many rabbits."

Love in Action Feedback
Collect all the fruit tonight and make up a group fruit basket. Choose someone to deliver it to a shut-in or homeless shelter this coming week.

As mentioned earlier, it can be especially effective to take the fruit to a non-Adventist acquaintance who is hurting, perhaps a neighbor or co-worker. You could also go to a nursing home and ask for the loneliest person there.

Ice Breaker
What is one of your greatest fears? Why? What helps you cope?

Group Activity: None this week.

Love in Action: None this week.

Leadership Tips
Note that the Group Activity in next week's lesson requires extra preparation prior to the meeting (cutting out squares, etc). Don't wait until the last minute.

If you are thinking of conducting another small group with this lesson series, this is a good time to start thinking about who could attend. Invite your current group members to start thinking about specific friends or relatives who might be in the next group. Have them make it a matter of prayer and encourage them to share their enthusiasm with another person.

It's also not too early to begin planning the group retreat to be held shortly after the lesson series is over. The retreat can be on a Friday evening or Sabbath afternoon. (See the manual for details in section III.2.h.) Be sure to invite members of any previous Body Building Groups.

13. Lesson: Lovesharing

Special Features

Learning to be a Group
It is helpful if discussion flows between group members rather than always being directed back to the group leader. Help to gently draw each other into the discussion.

Love in Action Feedback
How did the recipients of the fruit basket react?

Ice Breaker: None this week.

Group Activity
Matching Squares.

This game emphasizes teamwork and serving others. You need to put people together in groups of five each around small tables. If you have ten people in your Body Building Group you can have two groups of five. If there are people who are not in a group of five, use them as rule enforcers or play the game a second time and take turns. In the group of

five, each member will be given an envelope with pieces of a square in
it. The object of the game is for each player in a group to ultimately wind
up with a six-inch square. Using the cardboard from manila file folders,
cut out five squares measuring six inches on each side. Using a pencil,
mark the squares with lines and lower-case letters as follows:

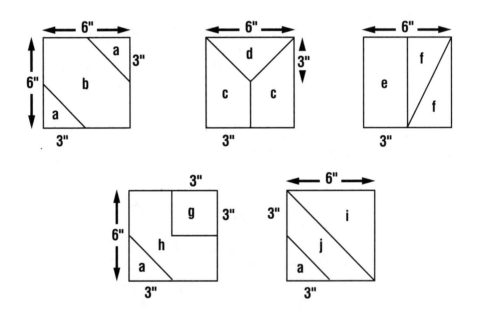

All the pieces marked "a" should be exactly the same size, the pieces
marked "c" should be the same size, and the pieces marked "f" should be
the same size. "By using multiples of three inches, several combinations
will be possible that will enable participants to form one or two squares,
but only one combination (of all the pieces) is possible that will form five
squares six inches by six inches" (*Joining Together*, David W. Johnson and
Frank Johnson, p. 325).

After drawing all the lines on the six-inch squares as indicated above and
labeling them with the lowercase letters, cut each square as marked into
smaller pieces to make the parts of the puzzle. Then mark five medium-
size envelopes A, B, C, D, and E. Distribute the cardboard pieces into the

five envelopes as follows:

Envelope A has pieces i, h, e.
Envelope B has pieces a, a, a, c.
Envelope C has pieces a, j.
Envelope D has pieces d, f.
Envelope E has pieces g, b, f, c.

"Erase the penciled lowercase letter from each piece and write on it, instead, its appropriate envelope letter (A-D). This re-labeling will make it easy to return the pieces to the proper envelope for later use when a group has completed the task" (*Joining Together*, p. 325).

Give each player one of the five envelopes. Before they open the envelopes, tell them that there are some very important rules:

1. The goal is for the group to make five separate squares of equal size. Each group member should wind up with a six-inch square that is just like all the rest.

2. The pieces have been mixed up, and no envelope has all the pieces for a complete square. The group members will have to exchange puzzle pieces to complete their squares.

3. You cannot take a puzzle piece from someone else; you can only give them away.

4. During the exercise there can be no talking, no pointing, no gesturing of any kind, no indicating what puzzle piece you want. You must either give pieces to others or wait for someone to give a piece to you.

These rules must be strictly enforced by observers. Now open the envelopes and begin. Time limit of 10 to 15 minutes.

After everyone has the same size square, you can ask the members what it felt like during the exercise and what lessons they learned. The main point of the lesson is that we can either

    a. Focus on our own needs at the expense of the team OR
    b. Focus on meeting the needs of others so that the team as a whole can be successful. I am successful as I make others successful.

Love in Action

Go to a shopping mall near your home this week. Sit down and observe the customers for half an hour. As you watch them pass by, ask yourself how your church could reach out to them more effectively with the love of Christ.

Done faithfully, this exercise can be a powerful eye-opener for a church that has tended to turn inward too much. Encourage people to do this exercise, and next week take time to debrief. Don't just say, "Go to a mall." Help them formulate specific kinds of issues they want to be thinking about as they observe people there. For instance, think about where different age groups shop the most. Use this as an illustration of how the same is true in church that one size or type does not fit all. Ask them to think about how the church's current activities are impacting these people's lives, if at all. How would these people feel if they visited your church next Sabbath?

14.   Lesson: Disciple Makers

Special Features

Learning to be a Group

Each member of the group is as responsible for how a particular meeting goes as is the group leader. It is a shared responsibility. Don't be a spectator. Invest in the success of your group.

Part of teaching the group to take "ownership" of group life is to refuse to be the "answer man" when questions or problems arise within a meeting. Throw it back on the group and ask what they think or how they would relate to a given situation.

Love in Action Feedback
Did you see some interesting people at the mall? (Hope you left the charge card home!) What did you feel as you watched these folks pass by?

Ice Breaker
Who was one of the most interesting or inspiring people you ever met? Why?

Tie this Ice Breaker into the theme for this week's lesson of "building people" through one person investing in another. We invest through our influence, association, mentoring, etc. This small group itself is a very effective method of building disciples for Christ.

Group Activity: None this week.

Love in Action
Be open enough to God's grace this week to respond to some hurt, slight, frustration, or put-down with unconditional love.

Have special prayer this week that God will truly bless the Love in Action during the next several days.

Leadership Tips
Remind group members to set aside time for the upcoming group retreat. You can also begin thinking about other ways the group may want to get together after the retreat. (Perhaps a group potluck once a month.) You could also examine the issue of re-contracting to continue the group in some form as described in Section V. 6 of the manual.

15.   Lesson: Just Imagine!

Special Features

Learning to be a Group
Come to the group in the spirit of a learner as well as a contributor. Be open

to what the Holy Spirit may want to teach you. Avoid being the "answer man."

Love in Action Feedback
Were you able to respond in new ways with unconditional love to some hurt or frustration this last week?

Ice Breaker: None this week.

Group Activity
Nine Dots.

This exercise illustrates the need for new solutions to old problems. It helps members see that sometimes they need to think outside their current framework to find better solutions. This activity illustrates the fact that the Body Building Lessons themselves present a vision of church that can help us break out of the walls of our mental box to find God's answers to today's challenges.

Make two copies of the following nine-dot pattern with no lines in it for each person in the group, plus a few extras. (See Appendix A for a full-page reproducible copy.)

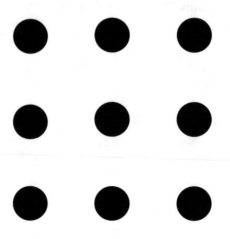

(From *Developing The Leader Within You*, John C. Maxwell, p. 80)

Give each person a copy of the nine dots with no lines, and a pencil. Tell them to connect the dots by making **four** straight lines without ever taking the pencil off of the paper. (Don't show them any solutions yet!) It can also be fun to let them work in pairs. (If someone has seen this game before, ask them not to let others know the solution.) After 3-5 minutes ask if anyone was able to do it. If not, show them how it is done by using the following solution:

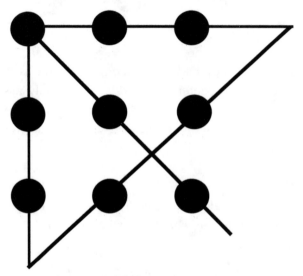

Ask them what preconceived ideas they had to overcome in order to solve the problem. One answer is that they had to overcome the idea that you have to stay within the area of the nine dots. You never said that in the instructions; they assumed it. To solve the problem you have to "color outside the lines," which we were taught as children never to do.

Now give them another copy of the nine dots with no lines on it and ask them to connect the dots using just **three** straight lines without taking their pencils off the paper. The solution is this:

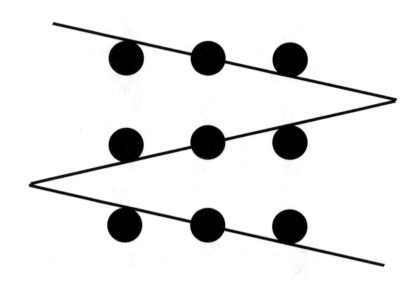

A preconceived idea they had to overcome this time is that you have to draw lines through the center of the dots. They only assumed that was true. Now you can again make the point that to implement God's vision for church we will also have to overcome some of our preconceived ideas of "how to be church."

Love in Action
Pray specifically this week that God will send at least one person to you who very much needs a listening ear. Keep your radar up!

16.   Lesson: The Value of Vision

Special Features

Learning to be a Group
The best way to get others excited about small groups is through your own personal testimony.

Love in Action Feedback
What hurting person were you able to carefully listen to this week?

Ice Breaker

As you look back over the past 16 weeks, what has been the most memorable moment or experience in this group for you?

Group Activity: None this week.

Love in Action: None this week.

Leadership Tips

Be sure to end the group experience with strong affirmation of people's involvement and growth. Celebrate the good things that have happened together during the past 16 weeks. Rejoice in the new dimensions of your vision of "church." This can be a great time to take out that list they made during the Group Activity in the second lesson. They were asked the two questions:

- What does your local church currently do very well?
- Where could your church improve the most?

Take the list and compare their perceptions at the beginning of this series with now and note any significant differences. Affirm the group life you've shared together. Make a mutual commitment to do what each one can to make God's vision a reality. Uplift them in a prayer of praise. Urge them to attend the group retreat. Finalize plans for agenda, food, etc.

V. Potential Outcomes

Don't just begin the Body Building Group without knowing where you are going. The following series of potential outcomes is derived from actual experiences of churches that used the Body Building materials. These ideas are not exhaustive, but they should spark your own creative thinking. Some of the outcomes will flow naturally from the Body Building Group experience. Others will require more careful planning, especially outcomes 5, 6, or 7. In either case, you will be more likely to achieve your purposes if you have thought them through ahead of time. Pick and choose from these seven outcomes according to what fits your circumstance and need. Because the lessons and small-group experience are designed to build a foundational vision, you can construct a variety of purposes on that foundation.

1. Fostering personal spiritual renewal.

The Body Building series can give new hope to Adventists who are stagnating in their Christian experience. Members who already have a vibrant relationship with God can find a deeper sense of calling and direction as well. A renewed sense of optimism and adventure can come as they study the breadth of God's plan and see how His intense, loving interest in building people permeates the Adventist church's message and mission. **Understanding this focus on personal renewal can help keep the Body Building Lessons from becoming just one more series of studies.** It keeps the focus squarely on both imparting information and energizing people through caring relationships. It also gives added value to the ministry among group members as they reach out to help each other understand and grow.

2. Developing a shared vision among leaders and influencers.

The Body Building Lessons plus the group experience can be a very effective way of instilling a new vision in the hearts and minds of your leaders and influencers. It can also be very helpful in building bonds of trust and understanding. Burt Nanus, in his inspiring book *Visionary Leadership*, comments on the value of vision:

> Vision is your key to leadership, and leadership is the key to organizational success. . . . Selecting and articulating the right vision, this powerful idea, is the toughest task and the truest test of great leadership. When this is achieved, the organization is already well on its way to the realization of the dream. . . . Developing and promulgating such a vision is the highest calling and truest purpose of leadership, for people instinctively follow the fellow who follows the dream. (*Visionary Leadership*, Burt Nanus. p. 7, 16, 19)

The Body Building series provides a rather unique opportunity for pastors to get close to their leadership over the 16-week period and discuss at length how to be church. It is from that open, caring, small-group environment that a true leadership team can often emerge with a common philosophy and vision for the future. One pastor recently commented that since his leaders went through the Body Building series, the atmosphere and attitudes on the church board have changed dramatically. Decisions are now made with the new vision of church in mind. **The pace at which you can pursue change will depend on the reaction of your leaders and influencers.** If only a few leaders support the principles and vision in the lessons, you will have to proceed more slowly, but that is at least a starting place on which to build broader support over time. Keep sharing God's vision in as many different ways as possible.

3. Reshaping the church culture by positively influencing values and attitudes.

Every church has a culture that is as real as the air we breathe. It can be defined as "what is important and what is permitted." It is the often-unspoken values, rules, and attitudes that dominate and permeate a congregation. The culture is made up of all the years of shared experiences in the church. It was there before the current pastor arrived, and it is ignored at a pastor's peril. The following are some sample cultural rules or norms that can inhibit change:

- Only longtime members can be in real leadership positions.
- Ordination makes the pastor different and more holy.
- Prayer meeting is sacred.
- The past is sacred.
- The order of church service is sacred.
- Risk-taking should be avoided.
- Information is more important than people
- Form is more important than function.
- Seating for Sabbath school must be in pews, not circles.
- We only play traditional hymns for church.
- The pastor should visit anyone who is in the hospital for any reason.

The list of norms can be endless, but they all have something in common: they are based on certain underlying values. **Once those values are altered, the rules and norms can begin to change as well**. The Body Building Lessons and group experience can have a very positive influence on those values and, therefore, on the culture. The lessons examine a number of negative cultural norms and values from churches that needed change. These are then contrasted with the genuine biblical principles and model.

Knowing ahead of time that one of your purposes with Body Building is to impact the church's culture can help you in at least a couple of ways. First, you can take time to think through what your own church's culture is like and then gently raise issues in the group about aspects of that culture that need to change. You can also make sure to recognize and reinforce those behaviors both inside and outside the group experience that are in harmony with the new paradigm and culture you are trying to create.

Another effective way to impact the culture through Body Building is to teach the Body Building Group members that they can become **missionaries to their own church.** If they buy into the philosophy contained in the lessons, tell them they can be like leaven among the congregation. Because of what they are learning, these group members now have the privilege of demonstrating a new degree of acceptance and caring toward fellow members. You want people who are not yet in Body Building to say, "Wow, if this is what Body Building does for people, then I can't wait to be in the next group!" Have special prayer and actually commission the group members to be sent out as missionaries to their own church. After conducting several Body Building Groups, this servant attitude can significantly improve the atmosphere of an entire congregation.

The Body Building Lessons can also be used to introduce new members to the culture you desire to instill in your church. Everyone who joins your church brings their own culture with them, whether they come in through baptism or transfer. If you want to build a new culture, you will have to become very intentional about exposing new members to the biblical vision of church.

The small-group retreat at the end of the lesson series will also have a positive impact on the church culture if you invite not only the current Body Building Group members but the members of all previous Body Building Groups as well. **Do this every time you finish a new Body Building Group.**

(A helpful book on cultural issues and systems is *The Equipping Pastor* by Stevens and Collins.)

4. Assimilating both new and veteran members into the Body of Christ.

The concept of assimilation is covered to some degree in the last part of the lesson "The Orchestra." You may want to review that material. When someone joins the church it is critical that they be well-assimilated into church life. This means they feel valued, needed, and a sense that they belong—socially, spiritually, and emotionally. Many members have never had that experience, or if they have, it was not sustained. Body Building can be a wonderful way to draw people into close relationship with others. Time and time again we hear stories of people who entered the Body Building Group as mere acquaintances and left as spiritual brothers and sisters. After one group was over, the head elder told his pastor, "God's timing must be perfect. If you hadn't invited me to join this group when you did, I would have left the church. I didn't tell anyone, but I had been desperately discouraged about church life. Now I have hope and feel like we've experienced right here, for the first time, what church is really supposed to be!" Another pastor invited to a Body Building Group a young couple who had only been coming to church three or four times a year. After 16 weeks in that close-knit group, their spiritual interest revived, they caught a new vision of God and of church, and they are now active in regular ministry.

Knowing ahead of time that one of your purposes is assimilation can help you target people. **One of the best ways to revive spiritual interest is to combine a few inactive or sporadic attenders in your group with more active members.** They can minister to each other and infect one another with new enthusiasm. That spirit is more caught than taught. Knowing your purpose also enables you to inject local stories (without names) of those who need assimilation into the group experience, to give the lessons as much relevance as possible.

(For an excellent book on assimilation see *Assimilating New Members*, Creative Leadership Series, Lyle E. Schaller, Abingdon Press.)

5. Transforming existing groups within the church.

In his book, *Prepare Your Church for the Future*, Carl George defines a healthy small group as one that has the following three elements: Learn, Love, and Do.

Learn—studying some material the group has chosen.
Love—providing mutual support and encouragement.
Do—giving attention to some aspect of service and ministry.

(The group also has a less prominent maintenance function, making decisions such as when and where to meet, etc.) These three legs of the stool must be in place in small groups in order to have balance. What distinguishes one group from another is the proportion of time and energy they give to these key elements. If a group focuses mainly on Learn, then we would call that a study group. If they focus mainly on Love, it is a support group. If they channel most of their effort toward Do, then they are a ministry or task group. All three elements are present in each group to different degrees as indicated in the following graphic:

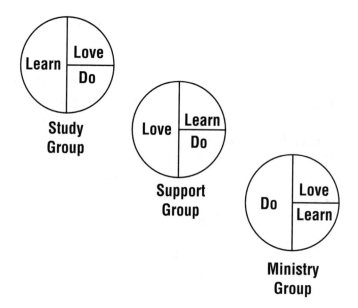

Many pastors wonder how to begin a small-group ministry in their church. If we define a small group as any face-to-face gathering of eight to twelve people who meet at least once a month, then you have several small groups in your church already:

• Church board

- School board
- Elders' meeting
- Deacons'/Deaconesses' meeting
- Adult Sabbath school classes
- Children's divisions of Sabbath school
- Pathfinders
- Social committee
- Finance committee

It may be that at present none of these is functioning as a healthy small group with the three key elements of Learn, Love, and Do. **But with a new vision, many of those existing groups can be transformed.** You can dramatically improve the level of care throughout your church by initially focusing on the small groups you already have. By knowing your purpose ahead of time, you can target existing groups in your church and invite them to join a Body Building Group. Over the next 16 weeks they can catch a new vision and be far more open to change.

As an example, in one church the deacons used to meet about once a month to work on the church building. They were a ministry or task group, focusing 100 percent on the Do element. The pastor realized that in order for the deacon group to live up to its full potential, they needed to somehow incorporate the two elements of Learn and Love. He decided to help them catch the vision of the Body Building series. After seeing that vision of what church can be, they decided to focus on the Love element by having breakfast together at a local restaurant before going over to work on the church. They ate in groups of four or five and talked about how things were going in one another's lives. This little meeting provided encouragement and support as each one shared. They also brought in the Learn element by meeting periodically to study topics that related to their ministry. The deacons are now experiencing a new level of vitality and closeness.

In another church the cradle roll division staff, consisting of four church members, was transformed into a very healthy small group. After attending a Body Building Group, the leader told me,

Now I see myself as the pastor of the men and women who work in cradle roll. I am a minister to them. With that new vision, I now have them over to my house for Sabbath dinner. We meet periodically to plan, but also to talk about our lives and how we feel about each other as a team. When they have problems, I try to offer a sympathetic, listening ear. I pray for them often. I really find my new ministry very fulfilling!

As you target existing groups, you will most likely not get everyone to join a Body Building Group, but even a few can have a transforming influence. Getting the leader of an existing group on board is the key. Suppose you have three adult Sabbath school classes. You invite the leaders and assistants to your next group. Only half join. A failure? Not at all. You now have 50 percent of your teachers who could transform their own classes from an exclusive emphasis on Learn to including the elements of Love and Do as well. They can then infect others over time.

6. Giving birth to new small groups.

For many Adventists, Body Building is their first experience in this type of small group. It is often the first time they have experienced church in such a highly relational way. Their support and enthusiasm can help immensely in launching a small-group ministry. In fact, it is not uncommon that when the 16 weeks of the Body Building Lessons are over, one or two group members will want to start their own group and invite their friends. You will obviously have to assess their readiness and ability to lead such a group, but this can be fertile ground for starting a small-group ministry. Rather than relying on such serendipitous happenings, you can be more intentional about using Body Building for starting small groups. Pastors have followed one or both of the following plans for finding new leaders:

a. **Choose a potential leader in advance and invite him or her to be your apprentice before the Body Building Group begins.** Explain that this invitation is tentative and you'll both need to reevaluate during and after the Body Building Group experience. Once the group starts, give the person increasing responsibility in the group, such as prayer, leading out in an Ice

Breaker or discussion question, or teaching certain portions of the lesson. Also invite the apprentice to meet with you every other week for personal training on how to lead a small group. Assign reading in a book on small-group leadership and go over it together. The Body Building Group becomes a laboratory. The best training is to follow Jesus' four-part sequence:

I do it, you watch.
We do it together.
You do it, I watch.
You do it by yourself.

    b. Another method is to **choose potential leaders in your mind ahead of time but don't tell them about that purpose until you have had opportunity to observe them in the small-group setting for several weeks.** You can still give them little responsibilities and see how they handle them and how they relate to others. If you still see potential, you can then ask them more formally to be an apprentice and enter training.

Having an apprentice keeps the pastor from getting locked into conducting all the Body Building groups himself. It is also more in harmony with the priesthood of all believers. The only way small groups can multiply is if the group leaders consistently strive to equip apprentices. Apprentice leaders can one day take their place in the body of Christ as shepherds who will in turn train others. Apprenticeship is almost a lost art within Adventism. As a result, there will be a very strong temptation on the part of Body Building Group leaders to handle everything themselves. They may feel that it is hard enough trying to lead out in a group, not to mention trying to train someone else at the same time. Actually, an apprentice can provide invaluable assistance during the group meetings and give insightful feedback after meetings. By working with an apprentice you will also grow much more quickly yourself.

One of the most pressing needs that can arise at the end of the Body Building Lessons is how the group can continue to meet. There is often a reluctance to break up after being together for 16 weeks. It is usually a good idea to give Body Building Group members the opportunity to **recontract** for another nine to ten weeks after the Body Building series is over. Group members can exit after the lessons are finished, or they can sign on again. No one should be made to feel like a second-class citizen if he or she doesn't continue. Keep the atmosphere upbeat and supportive. Even if there are only two or three who want to continue meeting, they can find seven or eight others and form a new Body Building Group. They may also choose to study other material or become a support group or ministry group. Either the pastor or apprentice can lead the continuing group, while the other can start an entirely new group. As the apprentice takes on a leadership role he can choose an apprentice of his own and keep the cycle going.

Remember, most small-group ministries fail because of inadequate training and support for new group leaders. **If you want to begin a small-group ministry in your church, start small.** It is better to go for quality than quantity. Better to build deep than wide.

(For an excellent resource see *How to Build A Small Groups Ministry,* Neal F. McBride, Navpress.)

7. Becoming the launching pad for a Ministry Development Process.

This section of the manual is certainly the most extensive and will require the most planning and organization. Potentially, there can be great rewards and benefits from pursuing this particular purpose and outcome consistently and well.

In order for the church to function effectively as Christ's body, church members must discover which part of that body the Holy Spirit wants each of them to be. Christians should find a ministry that provides for their own spiritual growth as well as the needs of others. They need to sense God's special calling and discover personal fulfillment and joy as one of His priests. Just filling a job or acting out of guilt will not do. Some studies indicate that up to 80 percent of church members nationally will not find an effective ministry on their own. They need to be guided and equipped. This presents church leadership with the imperative of setting up some type of process that makes sure that every willing person is involved in a satisfying ministry. **Ministry Development Process** is the name for the overall system that takes people step-by-step from noninvolvement to effective service for Christ.

There are several advantages to using a small group as the launching pad for spiritual gift development and ministry placement:

1. The small group becomes a living example of the body life people are studying about.
2. Group members know each other well enough to affirm one another's spiritual gifts.
3. The group can provide a supportive, caring environment in which to experiment with gifts.
4. The smaller size of the group facilitates more adequate follow-up.

As you think about establishing a Ministry Development Process in your church, remember **seven key steps** that need to be in place for it to work well:

1. Vision casting with leadership
2. Selecting Ministry Management Team
   a. Ministry Coordinator
   b. Ministry Placement Advisor(s)
   c. Information Manager
3. Choosing Assessment Guides
   a. Definitions
   b. When to use Assessments
   c. Member Profile
   d. Case Study
4. Establishing a Ministry Placement procedure
   a. Service Opportunity Descriptions
   b. Interviews

      c. Matching & Internships
5. Training
6. Recognition
7. Checkups

(Adapted from *Unleashing Your Church,* Dr. Paul Ford, p. 70, and *The Starter Kit,* by Leadership Training Network, p. 1-21.)

Each of these seven steps is explored more fully in the next section of the manual, Section VI.

VI. Seven Key Steps

The seven key steps that comprise the Ministry Development Process can make a fundamental difference in your church as the process becomes the feeder system for an expanding base of ministries. This particular outcome from Body Building will eventually affect everything you do as a church.

Step #1: Vision Casting with Leadership

It is vital that your church leaders endorse the concept of ministry placement based on spiritual gifts. The following steps have proven useful in enlisting leadership support:

a. Study the Body Building Lessons and Manual yourself.

b. Decide which leaders and influencers need to be in your first Body Building Group. Visit them personally in their homes to share the broad outlines of your vision for the future. Be sure to take the time to listen to their concerns for the church. Solicit their input and feedback. Help them feel part of the process. Give leaders and influencers top priority in your first Body Building Groups.

c. Invite the leaders to the Exploration Meeting and then the Body Building Group.

d. Promote the idea of the Ministry Development Process throughout the Body Building series.

e. After they complete the Body Building Lessons, have the leaders go through the Ministry Development Process themselves, including the assessments, interview, etc. It is very important that your leaders experience the process for themselves in order to see its benefits firsthand. The process may only be in a rudimentary form at this point, but take them through as much of it as possible to give them a taste.

f. If the leaders respond favorably, discuss the Ministry Development Process at an upcoming church board meeting and solicit their approval for setting up that process in the church on a pilot basis. It can be for a one-year trial period. Emphasize that you will start small and keep them regularly informed.

Step #2: Selecting the Ministry Management Team

The Ministry Management Team is responsible for the overall management of the ministries of the local church. It is directly responsible to the church board and is made up of the following:

- Ministry Coordinator
- Ministry Placement Advisors
- Information Manager

(Definitions for these positions will be explored below.)

The size of your team will depend on the needs of your church. In some churches the whole team can be made up of just a couple people who share responsibilities. In a larger church the team may have six or more members. Use the minimum organization necessary to accomplish your goals.

The team's specific responsibilities include:

1. Overseeing the Ministry Development Process
2. Educating church members regarding God's vision for church.
3. Developing a written description for every ministry position in the church.
4. Obtaining and cataloging information regarding each member's spiritual gifts and abilities.
5. Interviewing individuals and helping them discover a fulfilling ministry.
6. Providing training opportunities and resources.
7. Planning for regular encouragement and recognition.
8. Getting feedback from members in ministry to avoid burnout and discouragement.

The question naturally arises, "What is the relationship between the Ministry Management Team and the traditional nominating committee?" More than one type of scenario can be worked out. The one presented in this manual has the nominating committee retain its function of making the appointments to elective office. (The church board assumes that function in the interim.) These appointments are then voted on by the church in business session. This helps maintain a healthy system of checks and balances. The Ministry Management Team would then have the authority to place people in nonelective positions. Such appointments could be presented to the board periodically for review. A church may even want the board to have ultimate veto authority over the team's selections, although from a practical standpoint such authority would rarely be exercised in an atmosphere of trust and cooperation. Whenever the Ministry Management Team finds someone who needs to transition out of a church office, they should inform the church board and assist with locating a replacement. Even though the Ministry Management Team does not appoint people to elective office, they should still oversee all the training and support for those officers once they are in place.

Although the nominating committee would still function, its work would be modified in several respects:

- The nominating committee and/or church board would reduce the list of offices to be filled to an absolute minimum. Too often our people resources are siphoned off into responsibilities that do not actively involve ministry and exist only to perpetuate the institution. An office should be retained only if it directly contributes to the purpose and vision of the local church.

- The committee should understand that the institution exists to serve the members, not the other way around. They cannot fill positions by guilt or manipulation. People will have to be invited into office based on spiritual gifts, talents, conviction, and calling.

- The committee should work very closely with the Ministry Management Team, asking them for referrals and input.

Team Members:

a. Ministry Coordinator

The Ministry Coordinator chairs the Ministry Management Team and over-sees the entire process of placing and supporting people in ministry. This person should be committed to the doctrine of the priesthood of all believers and the vision contained in the Body Building Lessons. He or she should also have the gift of leadership and reasonably good organi-zational skills. The Ministry Coordinator is elected just like any other church officer and is also a regular member of the church board. There are at least two ways this position could relate to the traditional Personal Ministries Leader.

- Maintain both positions separately. Have the Personal Ministries Leader focus on planning outreach activities and the Ministry Coordinator on overall ministry management.

- Phase out the Personal Ministries position over time and replace it with the office of Ministry Coordinator. It is usually easier to bring about change through addition rather than subtraction, so this option could require patience to implement. If the current Personal Ministries Leader has the right aptitude, vision, and interest, make that person the Ministry Coordinator. (Merging the two positions and using the title Personal Ministries Leader would probably not be useful because that traditional name carries with it too many connotations from the past.)

b. Ministry Placement Advisor

The Ministry Placement Advisor is the person(s) who actually guides people, one on one, through the process of finding an appropriate ministry. They begin with gathering information from that person and discussing it with them in a personal interview. They advise them regarding potential areas of service. Finally, they shepherd people through the experimentation phase when they try different ministries and sort out which one is best for them.

The most critical link is the [Ministry Placement Advisors] who sit down with the members, interview them and coach them through the process. Selecting these mentors is the most important task. Training them can take months. The strength or weakness of any lay mobilization system rests on the quality of interviewers and mentors. (*The Starter Kit*, Leadership Training Network, p. 1-115)

It is helpful if the Ministry Placement Advisors have the spiritual gifts of Discernment and Exhortation (encouragement). They need to possess above-average interpersonal skills and be well-acquainted with spiritual gifts and body life concepts as well as the various ministry needs of the church.

Your attempts to establish a Ministry Development Process can run into a very serious roadblock unless the Ministry Placement Advisors are trained and functioning just as soon as possible. Without the Advisors, the pastor will have to do all the ministry placement interviews and help everyone find a ministry. To avoid this overload, the Advisors should be selected ahead of time, at least on a tentative basis, and invited to join the first Body Building Group. Their training can take place during the 16 weeks of the group meetings, on a different night. Some choose to meet every other week for training, while others meet less often for a more extended time. Some churches may find it useful to start training several weeks before the first Body Building Group begins. Trainees can practice on each other to begin with, plus a few guinea pigs you might hand pick. After the Body Building Group is over, the trainees can go with the pastor to help with the actual interviews and follow-up. Even finding and training just one Ministry Placement Advisor by the end of your first Body Building Group can be a big step forward. Try then to find another by the end of your next group and multiply as needed.

What should go into Ministry Placement Advisor training?

1. Review the subjects of spiritual gifts and priesthood of all believers.

2. Give an overview of the steps involved in taking someone from noninvolvement to effective ministry placement.
3. Explain how to gather appropriate information from the members through the Assessment Guides.
4. Discuss how to create new ministries.
5. Explore elements of a successful interview.
6. Discuss how to bridge people into ministry by contacting department heads and ministry leaders and setting up short-term internships.
7. How to schedule periodic checkups at three, six, and nine months.
8. Do role plays.
9. Take them with you on actual interviews.

For a more in-depth look at the role of the Ministry Placement Advisor, see Dr. Paul Ford's excellent book, *The Ministry Mentor Guide*. The address is 11805 Marquette NE, Albuquerque, NM 87123. Phone/Fax: 505-296-8568.

c. Information Manager

There will inevitably be a considerable quantity of information to keep track of in a well-run Ministry Development Process. At a minimum there are descriptions of all the ministry positions in the church and information on members' spiritual gifts and abilities. Creating a database on computer can be extremely helpful in sorting information and tracking needs. The Information Manager is responsible for creating and updating such a database. If a computer is not available or needed, a card file or notebook can be used. (*The Starter Kit* from Leadership Network in Tyler, Texas, has a very helpful list of software. See more information at the end of section VI.)

Step #3: Choosing Assessment Guides

a. Definitions

In order to help church members find God's will for their ministry, this manual provides the following Assessment Guides:

1. Spiritual Gifts Questionnaire
2. Ministry Experience
3. Abilities Review
4. Fulfillment Profile
5. Convictions Survey
6. Time Analysis

Plus the Temperament Inventory.

Copies of these assessments are located at the end of this manual in Appendix B (except the Temperament Inventory.) **They may all be photocopied for use in your church. Refer to the assessments in Appendix B as you read through the following definitions:**

Spiritual Gifts Questionnaire

The Johnson/Hunt Spiritual Gifts Questionnaire is rather self-explanatory. Go over the format of the questionnaire with the Body Building Group members after handing it out to see if there are any questions. Show how to transfer answers to the scoring sheet from the questionnaire. Remind people that all spiritual gifts tests are simply a starting place, an indicator and guide. They will need confirmation of their gifts from others and from their own sense of fulfillment as they experiment in ministry. Please note that the questionnaire itself does not include the important gifts of Healing, Craftsmanship, Music, and Prophecy. These four gifts are best identified by means other than a question-and-answer test.

Following the scoring sheet is a summary list of all the spiritual gifts in these lessons in alphabetic order with their definitions. You should give this list to the members, but not until after they have finished the Johnson/Hunt Questionnaire.

Ministry Experience

The term "ministry" is defined as *including* church offices. This assessment asks people to rate their current and previous ministry experiences.

They are asked how eager they would be to do that particular ministry again. You can affirm people in the ministries they enjoy. You will also need to transition people out of areas they do not like. Such transitions need to be made carefully but as quickly as possible. If the people who desire a change currently hold critical positions in the church that no one else seems able or willing to fill, you may have to invite them to continue for a while. Such a situation has high potential for burnout and needs a lot of support. You will also need to rotate that responsibility as much as possible. **Don't let people stay in a position very long that they do not enjoy**. It is better to rework how we do a certain ministry or delete it completely than to have people get worn out or resentful.

Abilities Review

In order to place people well we need to look at not only their spiritual gifts but their talents and abilities as well. The list on this assessment form is obviously not complete, so encourage people to write in whatever talents or abilities are not included. **Explain that it is not boasting to indicate what they do well**. Rather, it is a critical part of finding their place in the body of Christ. By "traits" we mean such things as being diligent, organized, innovative, creative, etc.

Fulfillment Profile

It is amazing how many Seventh-day Adventists think that church work is not necessarily supposed to be fulfilling. When asked to fill out this profile, one long-time church officer commented, "**I never thought of church work as being** *fulfilling* **before**. I just said 'yes' to what was expected in order to do my part. The various jobs in the church were simply needs that someone had to fill." Very little sense of calling and little joy. With such a low view of church work, is it any wonder that we have a hard time motivating people to get involved in ministry? Of course, ministry is not always peaches and cream, but it should be a fundamentally fulfilling experience. The Fulfillment Profile is an attempt to address that need. The assessment contains eight sets of pairs. Each of the items in a pair are somewhat opposites. People should score both items in each pair. If both the items in a pair score high, then that person's ministry could emphasize either one or both. If one answer is much stronger than the other, you will need to make sure that such a preference is reflected in the person's ministry. For instance, one church member circled a 5 for "Work primarily with things" and a 2 for "Work mainly with people." That reveals a clear preference, which could be very significant, especially if that person is heavily involved in people work. A change may be in order.

Convictions Survey

One of the real keys to motivating people for ministry is to find what service opportunities they feel strongly about. Tap into their own internal motivations. What grips them and stirs their emotions? What need do they feel convicted to fill? For instance, you would have no trouble motivating me to get involved in combating drunk driving. That is one of my purple passions in life. I would jump at the opportunity to help out. If you can uncover that type of inner conviction, you will have found a gold mine of energy. Service then becomes not just a job but a source of personal satisfaction. **People who minister in the area of their convictions have staying power**. Adventists are so used to simply filling positions out of a sense of duty that they may have a hard time at first getting in touch with their inner convictions. Be patient and listen well, probing gently to help get people's thinking started.

Time Analysis

It is often the case in churches that too few people are doing too much work. There are individuals who will consistently over-commit but never complain because it is the work of the Lord. The potential for frustration and eventual burnout are high. **It is very important that people not be overloaded**. Body Building tries to model balanced living. The Time Analysis can help you get a handle on whether or not people are doing too much. There may be members who are under-utilized as well. The point is to compare their actual time involvement with what they prefer it to be. That balance point will differ from person to person and vary during the seasons of life.

Your first one or two Body Building Groups will likely contain many of your church leaders. These people are prime candidates for some of the new roles that are so essential to restructuring how we do church. Yet these are also the very people who are shouldering the heaviest loads. Be careful. It would not be wise to give them new responsibilities without at the same time taking something of equal time commitment away. You will at some point need to make such transitions part of your planning.

Temperament Inventory [Not in Appendix]
This test can be an invaluable tool in the hands of a skilled Ministry Placement Advisor. For instance, having a person in up-front leadership who is 100 percent melancholy may be a red flag. They may prefer behind-the-scenes planning or detail work. If you put a 100 percent Phlegmatic in leadership of a Sabbath school division and give them a Choleric for an assistant you may be asking for trouble. The Choleric may be a real doer and the Phlegmatic more laid back. In such a scenario, the Choleric will be frustrated, and the Phlegmatic could feel threatened. Better perhaps to reverse roles. (Of course, there are always exceptions.) If you need greeters, you should probably look among the Sanguines. The Temperament Inventory can be the basis for an endless variety of helpful insights in strategizing how your members fit together to make up the body of Christ. (Temperament Tests and Scoring Templates can be ordered from Andrews University Press in Berrien Springs, Michigan.)

Caution! Many Seventh-day Adventists are not used to being tested for ministry placement. If you try to give them all of these assessments during or after the Body Building series, some people might resist. Although all of the assessment guides can provide helpful information, you will have to decide which ones to use. Don't over-test people! Do the minimum necessary to get them well-placed in ministry. Be sure to explain why the tests are given so that members can truly see their value. Remember that unless the people who take the test see how it will help them find a ministry, they will think it was a waste of time. Especially with new church members, it is important to get them involved in meaningful ministry as soon as possible. They can be reassigned later if necessary after they gain more knowledge and have completed more of the assessments.

b. When to use Assessments

There are various options for when to have members fill out the Assessment Guides:

1. Give some out during the 16 weeks of the Body Building Group meetings.
2. Give some out after the series is over, prior to the interview.
3. Fill it out with the person at the interview itself.
4. Don't use the actual assessment at the interview, but ask key questions from the assessment casually during the interview and then record the answers afterward.

The Spiritual Gifts Questionnaire should be given out on the night the Body Building Group studies "The Joy of Gifts" (even if you are not setting up a full Ministry Development Process). The Temperament Test could be taken around lesson 9 or 10. The Ministry Experience or Abilities Review could be given out toward the end of the group experience. The tests should be filled out at home and returned the next week. Allow some time for group members to talk about the results. Don't test without some type of follow-up.

After the Ministry Placement Advisors are trained and in place, it is helpful if they come to future Body Building Group meetings on the nights that any of the assessments are passed out. The Advisor can explain the purpose and process of testing and become better acquainted with group members. They can also give assurances regarding confidentiality. As the tests are collected, they should be reviewed by the group leader and then turned over to the Ministry Placement Advisor to be filed. The various test results should be kept in separate file folders for each person.

c. Member Profile

The results from each Assessment Guide should be transferred onto the Member Profile for quick reference. A sample Member Profile form is provided below and in Appendix B.

Member Profile

Name _____ Age _____ Ages of children _____

Years an Adventist ____ Years a member here ____ Sex: M F Marital Status: M S D

Time Analysis: Current hrs/month ____ Preferred hrs/month ____

Spiritual Gifts: Top three gifts and the score for each
 Gift _____ Score ____
 Gift _____ Score ____
 Gift _____ Score ____

Ministry Experience: Most satisfying ministries
 1.
 2.
 3.

Temperaments: (indicate score for each)
 Choleric _____ Melancholy ____ Sanguine ____ Phlegmatic ____

Abilities:
 1. Top four talents/hobbies
  a.
  b.
  c.
  d.
 2. Top three traits
  a.
  b.
  c.

Convictions: (Strongest convictions for ministry)

Support System: (Describe)

d. Case Study

At this point let's examine an imaginary case study that uses the Assessment Guides we have mentioned so far. Susan Moore is a 43-year-old nurse. She has a husband and three children ages 6, 9, and 11. She is a second-generation Adventist. Sue has two church responsibilities: clerk and teaching adult Sabbath school. She also helps out occasionally in Pathfinders, where her oldest son participates. By virtue of her office as clerk, she also serves on the church board. After she has filled out some of the Assessment Guides, we learn the following.

Time Analysis

Total hours per month	**27**
Preferred hours per month	**20**

Fulfillment Profile (partial)

Minister to adults	1	**(2)**	3	4	5
Minister to children	1	2	3	4	**(5)**
	Applies Little			Applies Strongly	

Ministry Experience

Ministry: _____ Clerk _____# Years __4__

1	(2)	3	4	5
Don't wish to do again				Would love to do again

Ministry: _____ Pathfinders _____# Years __1__

1	2	3	4	(5)
Don't wish to do again				Would love to do again

Ministry: _____ Adult Sabbath School Teacher _____# Years __2__

1	(2)	3	4	5
Don't wish to do again				Would love to do again

Her spiritual gifts are Encouragement and Teaching.

Her temperament is 60 percent Sanguine and 40 percent Melancholy.

The Conviction Survey indicated that she feels "a special burden for children who need to know how truly loving our heavenly Father really is."

Already we are learning a lot about Susan. Here are some preliminary thoughts,

1. She needs to cut back on her time commitment by at least seven hours per month.

2. The Fulfillment Profile indicates that she needs to be steered away from adult Sabbath school and/or the office of clerk, and into children's ministries. This is confirmed by the Ministry Experience test, where Susan reveals relatively low fulfillment as clerk and Sabbath school teacher but very high enjoyment in Pathfinders. Her spiritual gifts of Encouragement and Teaching could easily be used with children. Her temperament seems well-suited to working with young ones as well. The Abilities Review shows that Susan is very good with camping, crafts, and cooking. She could certainly teach these honors in Pathfinders. The Conviction Survey points in that direction as well. If Susan became part of the Pathfinder team, she would have a ready-made support system because the staff meets one hour before each meeting for discussion, prayer, and encouragement.

I can hear someone say, "But what if we can't find anyone else to be church clerk?" Remember, the church exists to serve the members, not the other way around. This is where we find out how serious we really are about operating the church based on gifts and not guilt.

Can you see how the various Assessment Guides can help get the best possible fit between member and ministry? When explaining the importance of these tests to our members, we need to emphasize how they enable us to make each Christian as effective in ministry as possible.

Step #4: Establishing a Ministry Placement Procedure

In this section we will explore several additional elements involved in placing people in the right ministry.

a. Service Opportunity Descriptions

A Service Opportunity Notebook is an integral part of the success of the interview and placement process. It provides a summary of what is involved in every ministry position in the church. Ideally this information would be kept in a computer database for easy retrieval and updating. A printout of each description should also be placed in a notebook where interviewees can look up the ministries they might be interested in. Don't simply adopt all the denominational ministry descriptions. Pick and choose and adapt. The Service Opportunity descriptions should be solicited from the people who are currently in those positions and then edited. Adapt them to your own needs. A simple Service Opportunity Description form such as the following could be used:

Service Opportunity Description

Position: _____

Responsible to:_____

Task/Responsibilities:

_____
_____
_____
_____
_____
_____

Ministry target:

_____
_____

Time commitment: Averages _____ hours per week/month

Availability: _____ Regular _____ Flexible

Spiritual gifts:_____
_____
_____

Talents/Abilities: _____
_____
_____

Related tasks/meetings:_____
_____

Comments:

b. Interviews

The following are some of the issues to keep in mind when conducting a ministry placement interview:

1. Meet face to face for about one hour in a quiet setting.
2. Ask open-ended questions that encourage people to share.
3. Be a good listener. Let them know you want to do everything possible to help them find a fulfilling ministry.
4. Affirm their gifts and abilities.
5. Emphasize balanced living and the fact that ministry involves all of life. Their ministry may be at work or home rather than in the church.
6. Be sensitive to the fact that they may be hurting and need to receive ministry for a while before they can give it.
7. Go over the results of the assessments, seeking to paint a coherent overall picture and pattern that can help them know how to invest their time and talent effectively.
8. Develop a specific Action Plan to follow in the next several weeks to get them moving toward effective ministry involvement. You may have to check back with them several times. Your Action Plan should include:
   a. **Who** should be contacted to get them started experimenting with ministry?
   b. **What** further training, help, support, information do they need?
   c. **When** are contacts to be made and followed up?

Keep one copy of that Action Plan for your records and give another copy to the person being interviewed. **It is vital that the Advisor follow through on whatever plan is agreed upon**. To fumble the ball here can result in discouragement and loss of interest.

Remember, the Ministry Placement Advisor does not determine someone's ministry. They simply help the person discover a ministry for themselves. The Advisor presents options and feedback, but ultimately it must be the Holy Spirit who guides people into selecting a particular ministry. If that selection is God's will, then it should eventually be confirmed by the body of Christ.

c. Matching & Internships

The Ministry Placement Advisor needs to be well acquainted with the Service Opportunity Notebook of existing ministries. The Advisor should have a list of potential ministries as well. Before the interview the Advisor should look over the assessment results he already has and determine what other tests might be needed. He can also begin to form a general direction for the interviewee's ministry. At the interview, the Advisor should present some ministry possibilities to discuss together. The goal at this point is to match them up with one or more potential ministries to explore. They will find final placement later. Create a sense of optimism, confidence, and adventure.

At the interview, the Ministry Placement Advisor can suggest any of four ministry options for each person:

1. Stay in current ministry
2. Substitute a new ministry for current one
3. Add a new ministry to current one
4. Begin ministering for the first time

If the interviewee wants to stay in his or her current ministry, the Advisor needs to discover the current level of fulfillment, motivation, and any need for training.

If the person wants to take on a different ministry and has narrowed the possibilities down to two or three, she should be asked if she would like to intern in any of those ministries for anywhere from 4 to 6 weeks. If so, start with the ministry that she finds most interesting. The Ministry Placement Advisor should then contact that ministry leader to let them know that the interviewee will be coming to learn about that ministry and give it a try. Such notification is preferably made in person or by phone.

One of the most critical links in the entire placement process is this contact with the ministry leader. It is helpful if the Ministry Placement Advisor explains to the ministry leader ahead of time what they hope will be accomplished during the internship and when the Advisor will contact the leader again for follow-up. The last thing you want is for the person who is exploring a new ministry to show up and be ignored or be made to sit on the sidelines. It is a good idea to make up a form that can be given to ministry leaders whenever someone is sent to them for an internship. The form could include basic information, such as the person's name, interests, spiritual gifts, talents, and what you hope will happen as a result of the visit.

If the person cannot find an existing ministry that interests him or her, the Advisor should take the time to help brainstorm possibilities. Create short-term assignments for experimentation.

The Advisor should stay in close contact with the interviewee until that person finds a niche in ministry. Once a placement is successfully made, the person's name should be turned over to the Ministry Management Team for further supervision and monitoring.

Step #5: Training

The Ministry Management Team oversees the training of volunteers. Ideally the church will find money to purchase resource materials and send people to appropriate seminars. Without adequate, ongoing training, it is hard for people to feel effective. The best training is on-the-job under the tutelage of a mentor who knows the ropes. The most helpful training is need-based, scratches where people itch, and has a problem-solving orientation. The team can solicit the help of ministry leaders and department heads to discover the training needs of the people under their supervision. Proper training sends the message that the church values its volunteers and cares about their success.

Step #6: Recognition

Christians do not serve in order to receive praise. Nonetheless, people still need to know they are appreciated. Appreciation is the oil that keeps the wheels of ministry turning. A church can provide such recognition in several ways. Leaders can intentionally and consistently catch people doing something right. You can also schedule recognition Sabbaths to mark special anniversaries in service and to celebrate when members find their own place in ministry. Recognition dinners are effective. You can rotate the appreciation and focus on different ministry groups throughout the year. Personal Encouragement/Appreciation Cards are also meaningful. The possibilities are endless. Unless a church plans for recognition, it can easily fall through the cracks. Why not make recognition someone's ministry?

Step #7: Checkups

Once members are placed in ministry, the Ministry Management Team will need to check back with them at least at three, six, and nine-month intervals during the first year. The checkup could be in the form of a visit, a survey, or both. You are making sure they are fulfilled and asking about any needs they may have for support or training. A system of checkups should also be in place for veteran members (at least once a year). You could meet with an entire ministry group and discuss their needs. It is also important to conduct exit interviews whenever someone leaves a ministry to discover the reasons for the change and to find out if the church failed to serve them in some way.

(See *Mobilizing Laity For Ministry*, W. Charles Arn, p. 57, and *The Starter Kit*, Leadership Training Network, p. 2-57.)

The following chart summarizes the main elements of the Ministry Development Process:

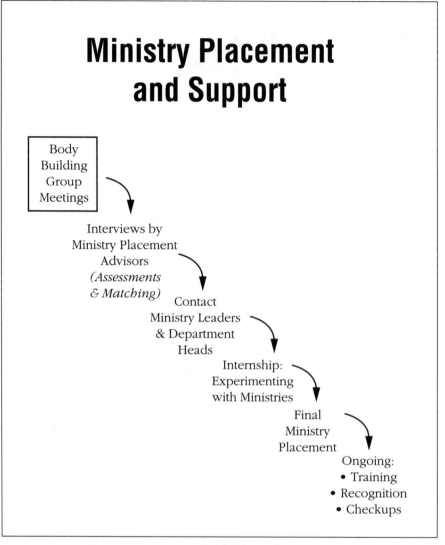

Ministry Placement and Support

Body Building Group Meetings

Interviews by Ministry Placement Advisors *(Assessments & Matching)*

Contact Ministry Leaders & Department Heads

Internship: Experimenting with Ministries

Final Ministry Placement

Ongoing:
• Training
• Recognition
• Checkups

As you contemplate setting up a Ministry Development Process, remember to start small and build. Make changes in bite-size pieces. **Pilot test your program and make refinements before going churchwide.** As you think about implementing, don't get so bogged down in the details that you lose sight of the forest for the trees. You may not be able to set up a full-scale Ministry Development Process at present, but do what you can to make improvements, keeping your eye on the goal. Remember also the two most crucial links in the Ministry Development Process:

1. Finding and training effective Ministry Placement Advisors and
2. Making sure that after the interview the person is properly handed off to the appropriate ministry leaders and department heads, who will help them experiment with various service opportunities.

Is usually a good idea to leave enough time between the end of one Body Building Group and the start of the next to adequately process graduates.

Caution! After studying about spiritual gifts in the Body Building Groups and taking the Spiritual Gifts Questionnaire, people will naturally have heightened expectations and want to start using their gifts in ministry. They will want to know where they fit best. Even if you do not plan on setting up a full Ministry Development Process at present, you should still try to help these graduates find a ministry. It may be as simple as giving them some of the Assessment Guides to fill out, then sitting down with them for an informal discussion of their needs and desires. Without some kind of follow-up, members can become disenchanted and begin to think that learning about spiritual gifts is just another intellectual exercise.

You may want to use some other material on spiritual gift implementation as a follow-up to the Body Building series later. The following resources could prove helpful.

Resources:

1. *The Starter Kit*
   Leadership Training Network
   PO Box 9100
   Tyler, TX 75711-9100
   Phone: 1-800-765-5323

The Starter Kit is a comprehensive compilation of the best thinking on ministry placement today. It covers such topics as The Leadership Team,

Choosing a Model For Your Church, Administrative Systems, The Interview Process.

2. *Connections*
Advent Source
5040 Prescott
Lincoln, NE 68506
1-800-328-0525

Connections is the Adventist version of the Networking materials that have been used so successfully at Willow Creek Church in Illinois. It teaches members about spiritual gifts through a seminar format and offers an in-depth, step-by-step system for gift implementation.

3. *Unleashing Your Church*
Dr. Paul Ford
11805 Marquette NE
Albuquerque, NM 87123
1-505-296-8568

Dr. Ford specializes in using small groups as a launching pad for spiritual gift mobilization. He is an international consultant on lay involvement with many years of experience. His materials include three workbooks: *Unleash Your Church, Getting Your Gifts In Gear,* and the *Ministry Mentor Guide.*

VII. Conclusion

As you reflect on the seven potential outcomes from the Body Building experience, you can see that some definitely require more preparation and planning than others. The following graphic illustrates the fact that increased planning is needed as you move down the list:

Potential Outcomes

Increasing Planning & Organizations

1. Fostering personal spiritual renewal
2. Developing a common vision among leaders and influencers.
3. Reshaping the church culture by positively influencing values/attitudes.
4. Assimilating both new and veteran members into the body of Christ.
5. Transforming existing groups within the church.
6. Giving birth to new small groups.
7. Becoming the launching pad for a ministry development process.

The last three outcomes on the list especially require planning ahead and "beginning with the end in mind."

You do not need to focus on any of these three outcomes to have a successful Body Building Group. They do, however, deserve careful attention at some point because those three deal with a vital aspect of church renewal—the way your church is organized and how your members function together. **The following chart illustrates how critical such an emphasis on organizational renewal is to church health. Examine the chart and the explanation that follows.**

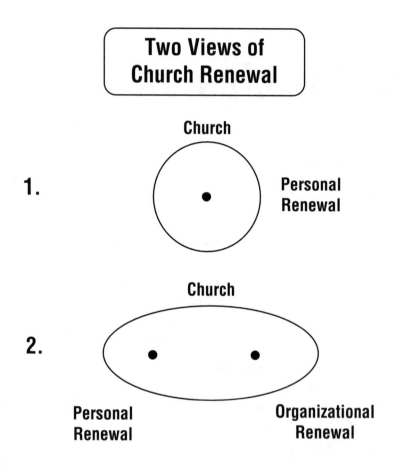

(Adapted from *Leadership* by Daniel A. Brown)

The above chart looks at two very different approaches to church renewal.

View #1 is a circle with one main emphasis at the center: "Personal" Renewal. It places the primary focus on renewing a church by revitalizing the individual members within it. That sounds logical but doesn't usually work. I have seen many pastors preach their hearts out and invest earnestly in members' spiritual growth, but when all is said and done, church has not changed very much. What is the problem? Their approach was imbalanced, too limited. Church is not just a collection of individuals.

It also has to do with how those people function together and how they are organized.

View #2 captures the proper dual emphasis. It sees church renewal not as a circle with one center but as an ellipse with two centers—"Personal" and "Organizational." In order for renewal to take root and have staying power, it must deal with both.

It is very difficult to sustain individual change unless at some point you deal with how we do church. The personal gains from the Body Building series can be dissipated over time unless we pay attention to organizational change along the way. Here are some examples:

- If members get excited about spiritual gifts and yet still have to deal with a nominating committee process that chooses people on the basis of guilt and manipulation, they could easily get discouraged.
- If someone knows their spiritual gifts but has no one who is able or willing to help them discover an effective ministry, they can fall by the way.
- Someone with the gift of leadership can become frustrated and disheartened if they are shut out by a church culture which requires them to pay their dues by being a member for five years before assuming any leadership role.
- New members with a first love experience can drop out if the church is not organized to assimilate them well.
- A member who is going through a time of personal pain and was encouraged by the Body Building experience can have nowhere to go for support when the Body Building Group is over.
- Members' enthusiasm for change can be lost if that energy is not channeled toward a clear vision and specific, tangible ministry goals.

If people graduate from a Body Building Group and are put back into business as usual, they can eventually lose heart and say, "Well nothing much has changed around here after all."

I remember one pastor whose strongest gift was teaching. He led several Body Building groups, and the members from each group were genuinely revitalized as they caught a new vision of church and their role as priests. However, as much as his members appreciated the Body Building experience, a number of them soon found their original enthusiasm slipping away. They needed the second half of that ellipse, "Organizational Renewal." This pastor did not have the spiritual gift of administration and could not see how to follow up his Body Building Groups. He need not have stumbled if he had brought into the process people who did have that gift, who could see the organizational road ahead. The pastor either needed to partner with these folks before the Body Building meetings or as soon as possible afterward. Once people with organizational gifts graduate from a Body Building Group, they can be formed into a Strategic Planning Team to oversee the organizational aspects of change.

Obviously it is not wise to tackle all seven of the potential outcomes at once. You would burn yourself out if you tried. **You can't do everything at once and must be selective**. As you contemplate the future, you need to be keenly aware of the various issues involved in church renewal and choose your outcomes wisely. Don't rush ahead without thinking it through. The more sincerely and intelligently we cooperate with God's plans, the more confident we can be of success in His eyes. The main factors to assess are your own strengths and weaknesses, the leadership resources available, and the current needs of your church.

Finally, don't let all the detail in this manual frighten you. Just do the best you can, and the Lord will undoubtedly bless. Use what you find helpful from the manual and go for it! **Remember, God specializes in using imperfect humanity. He can do marvelous things through you.**

Guidelines/Covenant

(reproducible)

Body Building Group Guidelines

1. I desire to become a mature, balanced disciple of Christ, growing in my relationship with God and effectively using my spiritual gifts and talents in ministries of love.
2. I am committed to giving the group high priority, sensing that God is willing and able to do something special for our church and for me personally.
3. I will set aside quality time to study each week's lesson in an unhurried manner and reflect on its meaning. I desire to minister to the other group members through my presence by regularly attending the weekly meeting and being on time.
4. I welcome the group's support and guidance in my attempt to understand God's vision for the church and my own life.
5. I commit myself to respect the views of other group members and maintain strict confidentiality regarding any personal information that is shared.

My Covenant

After reading the Body Building Group Guidelines, I accept the opportunity and challenge of being a responsible group member. By God's grace I will order my priorities in such a way that I can do my part in helping the group grow in its understanding of God's will and purpose. By word and example, I will endeavor to encourage group members in our mutual search for greater fulfillment and joy.

Signature _____ Date _____

Count The F's

FEATURE FILMS ARE THE RE-
SULT OF YEARS OF SCIENTI-
FIC STUDY COMBINED WITH
THE EXPERIENCE OF YEARS

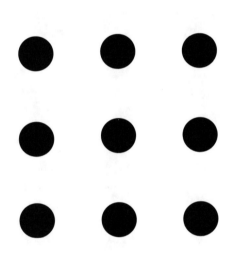

Appendix B
Assessments
(reproducible)

Service Opportunity Description

Position: _____

Responsible to:_____

Task/Responsibilities:_____

_____

_____

_____

_____

_____

Ministry Target: _____

_____

Time Commitment: Averages _____ hours per week/month

Availability: _____ Regular ___ Flexible

Spiritual Gifts:_____

_____

Talents/Abilities: _____

_____

_____

_____

_____

Related tasks/meetings:_____

_____

Comments:

Johnson/Hunt

Spiritual Gifts Questionnaire

Name _____ Date_____

Place either a 1, 2, 3, 4, or 5 on the line preceding each of the statements. You should answer according to how strongly you identify with that statement for your own life and to what extent it describes you. A "1" means you have very little sense of identification. A "5" means a strong personal identification. The numbers "2," "3," and "4" indicate degrees in between. (Your answers should reflect your life at present, not what you hope for in the future. Be frank and honest with yourself.)

Very little identification   **1   2   3   4   5**   Strong identification

_____ 1. I find it fulfilling to lend a hand behind the scenes for God.

_____ 2. I feel that opening my home to visitors and preparing meals for them is a ministry for me.

_____ 3. One of my first reactions to someone's need is to pray for them.

_____ 4. When it comes to meeting people's needs, I am comfortable helping those who are really "down and out."

_____ 5. People tell me that I am a good communicator.

_____ 6. I have unusual confidence in God's ability to meet people's needs.

_____ 7. It is very important to me that people feel appreciated.

_____ 8. I love to study God's Word very thoroughly and in depth.

_____ 9. People often seek me out for practical advice and value my perspective.

_____ 10. I enjoy directing projects and tasks in God's work.

_____ 11. I find fulfillment in stepping in and organizing projects.

_____ 12. I find real satisfaction in helping people grow in their spiritual experience.

_____ 13. I have a burning desire to share the Gospel.

_____ 14. I feel as though I have a God-given intuition about things.

_____ 15. I am very frustrated that I can't give a lot more money to the Lord's work.

_____ 16. Routine tasks such as setting up tables for church potluck, vacuuming rugs, folding bulletins, or cutting out felts, are enjoyable for me.

_____ 17. I care deeply that everyone feel welcome at church as part of God's family.

_____ 18. When I pray I hardly notice the passage of time.

_____ 19. I feel drawn to help people who suffer from addictions or emotional problems.

_____ 20. I am able to share biblical information in such a way that others learn.

_____ 21. I am often able to help people look beyond current difficulties to see how God can provide.

_____ 22. I would enjoy sending out thank-you cards to people who have given of themselves in some way for the church.

_____ 23. I enjoy searching out God's answers to challenging questions.

_____ 24. People say I have an unusually broad and mature perspective on life.

_____ 25. I am able to motivate and inspire people to get involved.

_____ 26. I enjoy planning and strategizing how to accomplish certain goals.

_____ 27. I think of myself as a "people person" and enjoy nurturing others.

_____ 28. I am able to discover people outside the body of Christ who have an interest in spiritual things.

_____ 29. I often seem to have a sixth sense about the rightness or wrongness of a certain course of action.

_____ 30. I feel that God is calling me to sacrifice financially for His cause, regardless of what others may contribute.

_____ 31. I like providing practical help, working with my hands to get a project done.

_____ 32. I feel a special burden to help meet the needs of homeless families.

_____ 33. I have seen God answer my prayers for others, sometimes in rather marked ways.

_____ 34. I often find myself ministering to people whom others seem to ignore.

_____ 35. I am often able to help people understand complex spiritual concepts more easily.

_____ 36. Difficulties only increase my trust in God, not diminish it.

_____ 37. I find great satisfaction in encouraging people who are hurting.

_____ 38. People tell me I have unusual insights into Scripture that they find helpful.

_____ 39. When individuals or groups are faced with several choices, I can often sense which one is best.

_____ 40. I am comfortable initiating various ideas and proposals.

_____ 41. I am comfortable with paperwork and details, as long as I can see how it will get us closer to achieving our goal.

_____ 42. People open up to me easily about their problems, especially spiritual needs.

_____ 43. Non-Christians respond positively when I talk to them about spiritual matters.

_____ 44. I am usually able to look beyond the surface to detect people's hidden feelings.

_____ 45. I receive special fulfillment from knowing that my funds are helping those in need.

_____ 46. I intentionally look for opportunities to help people around me in little ways that make life easier for them.

_____ 47. I feel called by God to minister through hospitality.

_____ 48. I know God has clearly worked through my prayers to help others.

_____ 49. I have a special desire to help the underdogs of our world.

_____ 50. I am able to explain to others how the Bible relates to their needs.

_____ 51. When others feel like giving up, I can still see possibilities with God.

_____ 52. In church I actively look around for people who seem to be lonely or discouraged.

_____ 53. People often come to me with their spiritual questions.

_____ 54. People say that God has given me unusual wisdom and good judgment.

_____ 55. I can effectively provide leadership in certain areas of church life.

_____ 56. I am able to coordinate the efforts and resources of various people to get a job done.

_____ 57. I find fulfillment in helping people discover their God-given abilities.

_____ 58. I find special joy in sharing my testimony for Christ with nonbelievers.

_____ 59. I am able to sense fairly accurately when someone's words don't match what is in their heart.

_____ 60. I love to give gifts, even if I have to go without myself.

_____ 61. I enjoy taking care of the little details in the church that others might overlook.

_____ 62. I desire to help people who go to bed hungry.

_____ 63. I sense God's presence most deeply through prayer.

_____ 64. I feel genuine compassion for disadvantaged people that society has cast aside and rejected.

_____ 65. I gain real fulfillment from sharing insights into God's Word.

_____ 66. I can maintain an unusual degree of hope even when others around me are terribly discouraged.

_____ 67. I sense God working through me when my comments and attitude brighten someone else's day.

_____ 68. I am not at all satisfied with cliche spiritual answers.

_____ 69. I am able to provide practical guidance so people can make good choices.

_____ 70. I would rather equip and train others to do a task than do it myself.

_____ 71. I like to analyze why certain programs aren't working and brainstorm how to fix them.

_____ 72. It is very satisfying for me to help people become effective in some area of Christian service.

_____ 73. It is relatively easy for me to turn conversations with non-Christians in a spiritual direction.

_____ 74. I can usually tell when someone has a "hidden agenda."

_____ 75. I gladly give away what I can of my own possessions to help those in need.

Please note that this questionnaire does not include the important spiritual gifts of Healing, Craftsmanship, Music, or Prophecy. These gifts are certainly as valuable as any other but can be identified best by means other than a question-and-answer test.

Spiritual Gifts

Scoring Sheet

Name _____ Date _____

Transfer your answers from each of the statements on the Spiritual Gifts Questionnaire to this sheet. Then add the numbers across in each row and place the total in the column at the right. After that step, circle your two or three highest scores. This will give you a starting place to discover your spiritual gifts. These gifts will need to be confirmed by others and by your own future ministry experience. (It is often helpful to have a spouse or close friend take the Questionnaire with you in mind. You can then find out whether they see you the way you see yourself.)

						Totals
Helps	1. ___	16. ___	31. ___	46. ___	61. ___	_____
Hospitality	2. ___	17. ___	32. ___	47. ___	62. ___	_____
Intercession	3. ___	18. ___	33. ___	48. ___	63. ___	_____
Mercy	4. ___	19. ___	34. ___	49. ___	64. ___	_____
Teaching	5. ___	20. ___	35. ___	50. ___	65. ___	_____
Faith	6. ___	21. ___	36. ___	51. ___	66. ___	_____
Encouragement	7. ___	22. ___	37. ___	52. ___	67. ___	_____
Knowledge	8. ___	23. ___	38. ___	53. ___	68. ___	_____
Wisdom	9. ___	24. ___	39. ___	54. ___	69. ___	_____
Leadership	10. ___	25. ___	40. ___	55. ___	70. ___	_____
Administration	11. ___	26. ___	41. ___	56. ___	71. ___	_____
Pastor	12. ___	27. ___	42. ___	57. ___	72. ___	_____
Evangelism	13. ___	28. ___	43. ___	58. ___	73. ___	_____
Discernment	14. ___	29. ___	44. ___	59. ___	74. ___	_____
Giving	15. ___	30. ___	45. ___	60. ___	75. ___	_____

Spiritual Gift Definition List

(In alphabetic order)

Administration
"The ability to organize and manage, working with and through others to achieve goals." (Bill Liversidge, *Principles of Church Growth*, p. 19)

Craftsmanship
"The divine enablement to creatively design and/or construct items to be used for ministry." (Bruce Bugbee, *What You Do Best in the Body of Christ*, p. 61)

Discernment
The special ability to distinguish spiritually between good and evil, genuine and false.

Encouragement
The special ability to encourage, console, and reassure members of the body of Christ.

Evangelism
"The ability to share the Gospel with unbelievers in such a way that men and women respond and become followers of Jesus Christ." (Paul Ford, *Discovering Spiritual Gifts*, p. 21D)

Faith
The ability to envision God's purposes and exhibit unusual confidence in His power to carry them out.

Giving

The special ability to cheerfully give material resources, with unusual personal sacrifice, in Christ's stead, to those in need.

Healing

"The divine enablement to be God's channel to restore people to health." (Bruce Bugbee, *Network*, p. 76)

Helps

The ability to meet the practical, everyday needs of others around you through selfless service and assistance.

Hospitality

Joyfully and cordially meeting people's physical and emotional needs particularly through food, lodging, and friendliness.

Intercession

The ability to gladly spend extended periods of time in prayer on behalf of others while exhibiting deep confidence in the workings of God.

Knowledge

The ability to understand biblical truth with unusual clarity and insight.

Leadership

"The special ability to set goals in accordance with God's purpose for the future and to communicate those goals to others in such a way that they voluntarily and harmoniously work together to accomplish those goals for the glory of God." (Peter Wagner, *Your Spiritual Gifts Can Help Your Church Grow*, p. 162)

Mercy

"The special God-given ability to feel genuine empathy and compassion for individuals, both Christian and non-Christian, who suffer distressing physical, mental or emotional problems, and to translate that compassion into cheerfully-done deeds that reflect Christ's love." (Peter Wagner, *Your Spiritual Gifts Can Help Your Church Grow*, p. 223)

Music
The special ability to glorify God and make Him known through the use of vocal or instrumental music.

Pastor
The special ability to guide, feed, and equip the members of the church in such a way that they develop a mature relationship with God and utilize their spiritual gifts in ministries of love.

Prophecy
The special ability to "receive divine revelations from God to be communicated to men." (Bill Liversidge, *Principles of Church Growth*, p. 20)

Teaching
"The ability to explain clearly and effectively apply the truth of the Word of God." (Leslie B. Flynn, *19 Gifts of the Spirit*, p. 74)

Wisdom
The ability to resolve life's problems and sort out difficult situations through the application of biblical truth.

Ministry Experience

Name _____ Date _____

What church ministries (including church offices) have you been involved in with this church or another in recent years? Begin with the most recent, including current ministries. Rate each by circling the most appropriate number. (Adapted from *Unleash Your Church*, Paul Ford, p. 200)

1. Ministry:_____ #Yrs ___

1	2	3	4	5
Don't wish to do again				Would love to do again

2. Ministry:_____ #Yrs ___

1	2	3	4	5
Don't wish to do again				Would love to do again

3. Ministry:_____ #Yrs ___

1	2	3	4	5
Don't wish to do again				Would love to do again

4. Ministry:_____ #Yrs ___

1	2	3	4	5
Don't wish to do again				Would love to do again

5. Ministry:_____ #Yrs ___

Abilities Review

Name _____ Date _____

1. Talents/Hobbies: We are eager to know what abilities you bring to the body of Christ. Check all of the following that fit you. Please add any of your talents/hobbies that are not listed. Circle the ones you like best.

_____ Administration/Management	_____ Information systems
_____ Advertising	_____ Janitorial
_____ Artistic painting	_____ Landscaping
_____ Audio/visual	_____ Leadership
_____ Auto repair	_____ Legal
_____ Bookkeeping	_____ Library skills
_____ Camping	_____ Lighting/Electrical
_____ Carpentry	_____ Marketing
_____ Coaching	_____ Musical instrument
_____ Collecting	_____ Planning/Problem solving
_____ Cooking	_____ Playing athletics
_____ Computers	_____ Plumbing/Heating
_____ Communications	_____ Printing/Layout
_____ Counseling	_____ Sewing
_____ Arts/Crafts	_____ Singing
_____ Drama	_____ Teaching
_____ Floral arrangements	_____ Typing/Secretarial
_____ Gardening/groundskeeping	_____ Water activities
_____ Giving speeches	_____ Woodworking
_____ Office skills	_____ Working with handicapped
_____ Health/Medical	_____ Writing
_____ Hiking	_____ Other:
_____ Hospitality	_____ Other:
_____ Interior decorating	_____ Other:

2. Traits: Please list two of your strongest traits or characteristics.

a.

b.

Fulfillment Profile

Name _____ Date _____

This sheet contains eight pairs of related statements. Answer both statements in each pair. Circle either a 1, 2, 3, 4, or 5 depending on how strongly that statement applies to who you are and what you want for your own ministry. A "1" means that the statement applies to you very little. A "5" means that it strongly applies to you. The numbers "2," "3," and "4" are degrees in between. Each statement begins with the words, "I like to. . . ." (There is no final scoring. We are simply looking for self-understanding.)

	Applies Little				Applies Strongly
I Like To . . .					
Minister as part of team or group.	1	2	3	4	5
Minister on my own as an individual.	1	2	3	4	5
Minister within the church to members.	1	2	3	4	5
Minister outside the church to nonmembers.	1	2	3	4	5
Be involved in planning and organizing.	1	2	3	4	5
Be involved in doing and implementation.	1	2	3	4	5
Lead out in a ministry.	1	2	3	4	5
Be a follower.	1	2	3	4	5
Work primarily with things.	1	2	3	4	5
Work mainly with people.	1	2	3	4	5
Be self-directed.	1	2	3	4	5
Be directed by others.	1	2	3	4	5
Minister to adults.	1	2	3	4	5
Minister to children.	1	2	3	4	5
Be involved on a regular basis.	1	2	3	4	5
Be involved occasionally.	1	2	3	4	5

Conviction Survey

Name _____ Date _____

The conviction survey gives you an opportunity to reflect on what desire(s) for service God may be laying on your heart. An area of conviction is a ministry you find highly motivating and would love to get involved with. It may exist now or need to be created. Your inner conviction may be for service within the church or without. It may be for certain groups of people, such as teenagers, baby boomers, or the handicapped.

1. I have the greatest concern for: (circle one)

Infants	Singles
Children	Young couples
Teens	Elderly
Handicapped	Baby boomers
Addicts	Other:

2. Please fill out parts A and/or B according to what applies best to you:
   A. The greatest need(s) in the **church** that I wish I could help with is:

   B. The greatest need(s) in **society** that I wish I could help with is:

3. If I had a million dollars, I would give it away for the following one or two specific needs:

Time Analysis

Name _____ Date _____

Current church offices held:

    1._____ Hours per month (Aver) _____

    2._____ Hours per month (Aver) _____

    3._____ Hours per month (Aver) _____

Current ministries other than church offices:

    1._____ Hours per month (Aver) _____

    2._____ Hours per month (Aver) _____

    3._____ Hours per month (Aver) _____

Current committees:

    1._____ Hours per month (Aver) _____

    2._____ Hours per month (Aver) _____

    3._____ Hours per month (Aver) _____

Other:

    1._____ Hours per month (Aver) _____

    2._____ Hours per month (Aver) _____

Total actual hours per month (add numbers above): _____

Total preferred hours per month: _____

Member Profile

Name _____ Date _____

Years an Adventist ____ Years a member here ____ Sex: M F Marital Status: M S D

Time Analysis: Current hrs/month ____ Preferred hrs/month ____

Spiritual Gifts: Top three gifts and the score for each:
     Gift _____ Score ____
     Gift _____ Score ____
     Gift _____ Score ____

Ministry Experience: Most satisfying ministries:
     1.
     2.
     3.

Temperaments: (indicate score for each)
     Choleric_____ Melancholy____ Sanguine ____ Phlegmatic ____

Abilities:
     1.Top four talents/hobbies
     a.
     b.
     c.
     d.
     2.Top three traits/characteristics
     a.
     b.
     c.

Convictions: (Strongest convictions for ministry)

Support System: (Describe)